Coast to Coast

the Wainwright route
St Bees to Robin Hood's Bay

Sandra Bardwell

Rucksack Readers

Coast to Coast the Wainwright route

Published 2010 by Rucksack Readers, Landrick Lodge, Dunblane, FK15 0HY, UK

Telephone +44/0 1786 824 696, fax +44/0 1786 825 090
Email info@rucsacs.com, website **www.rucsacs.com**

British Library cataloguing in publication data: a catalogue record for this book is available from the British Library.

ISBN 978-1-898481-34-8

Designed in Scotland by **WorkHorse** (www.workhorse.co.uk)
Printed in China by Hong Kong Graphics & Printing Ltd on waterproof, biodegradable paper

Title page photograph: Above Carlton Bank from the Coast to Coast

Publisher's note

All information was checked prior to publication. However, changes are likely: follow waymarkers carefully and always be vigilant for diversions and alterations. Before setting out, walkers are advised to check online for updates: useful links are provided on our website at **www.rucsacs.com/Coast-to-Coast.**

Parts of the route are wet underfoot, others rough and rocky. Navigation requires care: waymarking is very variable and often sparse; you need map and compass skills, especially over high ground and in mist or low cloud. You are responsible for your own safety: make sure that your clothing, food and equipment are suited to your needs and that your intended walk can be safely completed in daylight. The publisher cannot accept any liability for any ill-health, injury or loss arising directly or indirectly from reading this book.

Feedback is welcome and will be rewarded

All feedback will be followed up, and readers whose comments lead to changes will be entitled to claim a free copy of our next edition upon publication. Please send emails to **info@rucsacs.com**

Coast to Coast: contents

Introduction

The Coast to Coast walk follows a magnificently varied 184 miles (296 km) route across northern England. Originally devised, walked and promoted by Alfred Wainwright, it has become Britain's most popular long-distance walk.

Between St Bees and Robin Hood's Bay, with their dramatic sea cliffs, the walk takes you through the finest landscapes in northern England. It traverses three national parks: the rugged mountains of the Lake District, green and peaceful Swaledale in the Yorkshire Dales, and the rolling heathery ridges of North York Moors. You pass historic churches, mining relics, and many other reminders of the history of settlement in the towns, villages and countryside. The walk follows superbly built paths across open moors and fells, winds around barley fields and along clifftop paths, and leads along former coffin routes, a disused railway and quiet roads. The Coast to Coast is easily accessible by public transport and is blessed with a wealth of accommodation, tempting tea rooms and inviting pubs.

Highlights among the wide-ranging views include the Irish Sea and the Isle of Man from St Bees Head; the Lake District hills from Dent in the west and, much later, from the Pennine watershed on Nine Standards; the North York Moors drawing closer in the Vale of Mowbray; and the first sight of the North Sea approaching High Hawsker.

The dales and valleys are places of quiet beauty: Smardale, with its old bridge and viaduct, and the barns and stone walls of Swaledale. Villages such as Keld, Bolton-on-Swale and Littlebeck blend with the landscape. Natural features include St Bees Head crowded with sea birds, the Borrowdale woods, limestone pavements beyond Shap, the purple heather-clad North York Moors, hay meadows and ubiquitous skylarks. But what makes the Coast to Coast walk special, perhaps unique, is the spontaneous camaraderie among fellow walkers – the ready sharing of advice, offers of assistance and good fellowship.

Across Ennerdale to Lake District fells

Planning and preparation

The Coast to Coast (C2C) uses a wide variety of routes throughout its length. You'll follow narrow paths beside and across fields, well-used mountain paths, farm roads, old trackways through mining areas and woodlands, moorland tracks (often boggy), and coastal clifftop paths. It also uses historic routes, notably an old railway trackbed between Bloworth Crossing and the Lion Inn on Blakey Ridge.

Generally these paths are either public footpaths or bridleways, or permissive paths – routes where access is not by right but by permission of the landowner. There are also stretches of minor road, usually flanked by a grassy verge and with good visibility for oncoming traffic. Almost all of these are less than half a mile long, the exception being the 3 miles (5 km) from the Lion Inn north and eastwards.

Accommodation and facilities

Fortunately the route passes through many villages and small towns where you will find a wide range of accommodation, places to eat and drink and usually also a shop. Consequently you don't need to allow for much extra walking to reach a bed for the night. Some accommodation providers, especially those serving isolated locations (such as Clay Bank Top), will pick you up at the end of the day and take you back to the start of the next day's walk.

The table opposite shows what was available at various places along the route when this book was finalised (autumn 2009). It's presented to help you plan your accommodation choices, with guidance also on food and drink and other facilities. It's not exhaustive, and there are various places on and near the route with accommodation only: for example Tarnflatt Hall (near St Bees Head) and East Applegarth (west of mile 111) each has a camping barn, and Marrick (mile 106) has a B&B.

Egton Banks Farm B&B

Facilities along the route

	miles from last place	km from last place	café, pub, restaurant	shop	campsite	hostel, barn, bunkhouse	B&B, hotel	toilets	ATM
St Bees			✓	✓	✓		✓	✓	✓
Sandwith	5	8	✓				✓		
Cleator	4	6½	✓	✓			✓		
Ennerdale Bridge	5	8	✓	✓	✓		✓		
Ennerdale YH (Gillerthwaite)	6	10				✓			
Black Sail YH	4	6½				✓			
Honister Slate Mine	3	5	✓			✓		✓	
Seatoller	1½	2½	✓		✓		✓	✓	
Rosthwaite	2	3	✓	✓	✓	✓	✓	✓	
Grasmere	7½	12	✓	✓	✓	✓	✓		✓
Patterdale	6½	10	✓	✓	✓	✓	✓	✓	
Shap	15½	25	✓	✓	✓	✓	✓		✓
Orton	8	13	✓	✓	✓		✓		
Newbiggin-on-Lune	6	10	✓		✓	✓	✓		
Kirkby Stephen	7½	12	✓	✓	✓	✓	✓	✓	✓
Keld	11	18	✓		✓	✓	✓		
Reeth	10½	17	✓	✓	✓	✓	✓	✓	✓
Richmond	10½	17	✓	✓		✓	✓	✓	✓
Colburn	2½	4	✓				✓		
Brompton-on-Swale	2	3	✓	✓		✓	✓		✓
Bolton-on-Swale	2½	4	✓				✓		
Danby Wiske	7	11	✓		✓		✓		
Oaktree Hill	2	3			✓	✓	✓		
Ingleby Cross	6½	10	✓		✓		✓		
Lord Stones (Carlton Bank)	8½	14	✓		✓			✓	
Clay Bank Top	3½	6			✓		✓		
Blakey Ridge	9	14	✓		✓		✓		
Glaisdale	8½	14	✓	✓			✓	✓	
Egton Bridge	2½	4	✓				✓		
Grosmont	1½	2	✓	✓	✓		✓	✓	✓
Littlebeck	4	6½			✓		✓		
High Hawsker	6½	10	✓		✓		✓		
Robin Hood's Bay	4	6	✓	✓	✓	✓	✓	✓	✓

Table correct at time of publication

About a mile off-route beyond Ingleby Cross (see page 91), Osmotherley has various food options (pubs and a shop) plus a range of accommodation (B&Bs, and a nearby youth hostel and campsite). Muker and Gunnerside are on the low-level route through Swaledale: see page 75. Each has B&B accommodation and a pub for meals; Muker also has a small shop.

Accommodation varies widely in price, from campsites at under £5 per person to hotels at well over £50, although the choice is limited in some places. It's wise to book ahead to ensure that you don't

The Blue Bell, Ingleby Cross

have to compromise your preferences or your bank balance. This applies particularly to the busy summer season: in some key places accommodation of any kind may simply be full.

Weekends can be tricky: supplements may be added to weekday tariffs and single night bookings may not be accepted, particularly in Robin Hood's Bay. Bear in mind that few B&Bs have genuine single rooms and solo walkers usually have to pay a supplement. Also, some camping barns will not accept bookings for individuals at weekends. Various websites and publications provide useful information: see pages 110 and 111.

To keep costs down, consider staying at hostels. The Youth Hostel Association runs several hostels in the Lake District, and at Kirkby Stephen, Grinton (near Reeth), Cote Ghyll (near Osmotherley) and Boggle Hole (1 mile south of Robin Hood's Bay). Meals are available, as well as dormitories or private rooms, bathrooms and a communal kitchen. Some have internet access and other facilities. Some may be closed between 10.00 and 17.00.

Black Sail Youth Hostel: see page 46

The Association also operates camping barns (fairly basic hostels) scattered along the walk. For most of these you need to bring a sleeping bag. They are equipped with a kitchen, and sleeping areas are communal. There are also a few privately-run barns.

For further information consult the sources listed in Part 4 under specialist websites and Accommodation contacts. Alternatively, sign up with a tour operator featuring the walk. Most will transfer your overnight baggage between accommodations: see page 110.

If you're happy to carry a tent, sleeping bag, food and cooking equipment, and to cope with bad weather, you can economise by camping independently. There are commercial campsites with facilities in many places and a few pubs allow camping in their grounds. Camping is not permitted at youth hostels. Wild camping is generally not encouraged but if you choose to do so, ask the landowner's permission if possible, and camp discreetly. Remember to purify water drawn from streams. Follow the widely accepted Camping Code: see panel above.

Camping Code

✓ *Ask permission from the landowner before camping wild*

✓ *Camp discreetly away from roads, houses, popular sites*

✓ *Move on after one night*

✓ *Use only a camp stove, never light a fire*

✓ *Help to keep water supplies pure and clean*

✓ *Bury human waste completely, at least 30m away from streams or paths*

✓ *Remove all litter*

✓ *Leave no trace of your pitch*

Walker's tent near Bloworth Crossing (April)

9

Waymarking

Unlike National Trails such as the Pennine and Cleveland Ways which are signed with a standard acorn logo, there is no consistent system of waymarking for this route. Wooden finger boards with the words 'Coast to Coast' (sometimes 'C to C' or 'C2C' are fairly common), but don't expect to find such signs anywhere in Lake District National Park. There you need to navigate by the features of each day's walk.

You will also meet home-made, informal signs, such as the welcome one at Burnbanks near Haweswater Reservoir, just outside Lake District National Park. The walk follows the Cleveland Way between miles 138 and 151 (see maps on pages 91, 93 and 95), and along the final clifftop section into Robin Hood's Bay: see page 105. Follow the acorn waymarkers on these sections.

On the moorland between Kirkby Stephen and Keld (Section 7), three seasonal routes have been defined by Yorkshire Dales National Park to try to minimise erosion of the fragile peatlands. Follow the coloured waymarkers: red (from May to July), blue (August to November), and green (December to April, and in bad weather). They are all described on pages 64-9 and clearly shown on the maps.

Some sections of the route through farmland follow an intricate chain of paths separated by stiles and gates. While most are clearly marked, you still need to check the map and notes frequently to ensure that you don't stray from the route – possibly onto land where you may not be welcome. It's easy to miss a turning because of a vandalised sign, or you may be distracted by good views or interesting conversation.

Above: the route follows the Cleveland Way in places
The rest: C2C signage, where present, varies in style and age

As a rule of thumb, if you haven't seen a waymarker for about 15 minutes, or if you reach an unmarked junction, you may well have come adrift. If in doubt, retrace your steps until you find a marker. Avoid the temptation to cut cross-country in the hope of picking up the route.

How long will it take?

Most walkers complete the full distance of 184 miles (296 km) in 12 to 16 days of walking. Part 3 presents the walk in 15 sections, each one a feasible day's walk for most people. However some fit and hardy folk complete it in as few as 8 days, and others spread it over as many as 20. Check the altitude profiles and maps for each section before deciding.

		miles	km	map pages
1	St Bees to Ennerdale Bridge	14	22·5	41, 43
2	Ennerdale Bridge to Rosthwaite	16½	26·5	45, 47
3	Rosthwaite to Patterdale	14	22·5	49, 51
4	Patterdale to Shap	15½	24·9	53, 55
5	Shap to Orton	8	12·9	59
6	Orton to Kirkby Stephen	13½	21·7	61, 63
7	Kirkby Stephen to Keld	11	17·7	65, 67
8	Keld to Reeth	10½	16·9	71, 73
9	Reeth to Richmond	10½	16·9	77, 79
10	Richmond to Danby Wiske	14	22·5	83, 85
11	Danby Wiske to Ingleby Cross	8½	13·7	89, 91
12	Ingleby Cross to Clay Bank Top	12	19·3	91, 93, 95
13	Clay Bank Top to Blakey Ridge	9	14·5	95, 97
14	Blakey Ridge to Grosmont	12½	20·1	99, 101
15	Grosmont to Robin Hood's Bay	14½	23·3	103, 105
	Total	184	296	

The table shows distances for a 15-day walk. If you combine sections 5 and 6, you could make a 14-day walk at the price of a 21.5-mile (35 km) fifth day. Conversely, if you split Section 3 into two, you would need 16 days but could enjoy a break at Grasmere. There's lots of accommodation throughout the route, so itineraries are easy to plan, especially if you are flexible about where you sleep.

You may like to take a little extra time to follow some or all of the rituals associated with the C2C. You can dip the toe of your boot (or your bare toes) in the sea at St Bees. Later, at Robin Hood's Bay, follow Wainwright's instructions: 'Go forward and put your boot in the first salt-water puddle. By this ritual you will have completed a walk from one side of England to the other.' By tradition, some carry a pebble from St Bees' shore and deposit it on the beach at Robin Hood's Bay – to mystify future geologists! And there's a C2C log book you can sign in the Wainwright Bar of the Bay Hotel on the sea front.

Saturday is the most popular starting day, so it's prudent to book accommodation well in advance. Bear in mind that most providers in Robin Hood's Bay will not take bookings for just one night at weekends, and the weekend tariff may be higher than that for weekdays.

You can split your walk into two or more separate trips. The best break points for this purpose are Kirkby Stephen and Richmond: these have good public transport connections, and at least two companies offer minibus transfers and car parking to simplify the logistics, with an option to link with mainline rail to/from Darlington Station: see page 110.

Throughout this book we give distances in miles with kilometre equivalents. The maps have scale bars in both units, but to avoid clutter, distances along the route are shown by red mileage dots alone. For short distances in directions, we use metres: a metre is only 10% longer than a yard and you won't go astray if you start looking for a turning slightly too soon. For example, 50 m is actually 55 yards and 100 m is 109 yards.

Each end of the route is clearly marked: there's a stone pillar and information board overlooking St Bees beach, and a sign outside the Bay Hotel on the seafront at Robin Hood's Bay. Although signage, websites and other guidebooks quote the route's length as anywhere between 182 and 192 miles, our section distances have all been measured accurately, and they add up to 184 miles/296 km. Let that not belittle the task: in practice, including diversions for food and accommodation, most walkers will cover 190-200 miles.

Which direction?

The vast majority of walkers travel from west to east, as the signs at St Bees and Robin Hood's Bay suggest. The prevailing winds tend to come from the west, and this puts them behind you. Formal waymarkers recognise that walkers travel in both directions, although the informal ones often do not. Our advice is to follow the founder's footsteps eastwards.

Elevation and pace

The walk involves a total ascent of about 7000 m (23,000 ft). A high proportion of this challenge confronts you in the Lake District, but be prepared also for short, steep climbs, often in quick succession, across the North York Moors. The altitude profiles at the start of each section are all shown to the same scale. They underline some sharp contrasts in the gradient and altitude gain between different sections.

Depending on the season and recent weather, many sections of the route may be boggy, in places very boggy, especially across moorland. Some paths in the Lake District are rough and rocky and cannot safely be taken at normal walking pace.

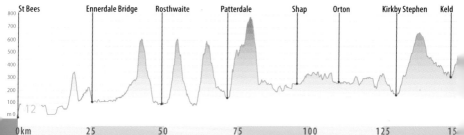

12

Cairn at Nine Standards (661m/2170ft)

Another factor influencing your rate of travel will be the number of people in your group. Groups travel at the pace of their slowest member, or slightly less. Overall, expect to average 2 to 2½ mph (3-4 km/hr) unless you're very fit and keen to press on.

What is the best time of the year?

From late October to late March isn't the best time to do this walk – unless you live locally and can seize opportunities of good weather at short notice. In winter, snow and ice are likely, especially in the Lake District, and bitterly cold winds sweep across exposed ground. In addition, hours of daylight are short between November and January. Midwinter days may have as few as 8 hours of daylight, whereas in midsummer the light may last for 16 hours or more. The combination of winter factors can make the walk unduly difficult, or even dangerous. Bear in mind that October to January are the wettest months and April to July the driest. Also, many accommodations are closed in winter.

Between June and September, accommodation may also be difficult to find if you haven't booked well ahead, particularly for solo walkers seeking B&Bs or hotels. From mid-June to late September many paths, particularly along field edges, may be partly overgrown and less obvious. If you wear shorts, beware of nettles and brambles. All in all, the ideal months are May, June and September.

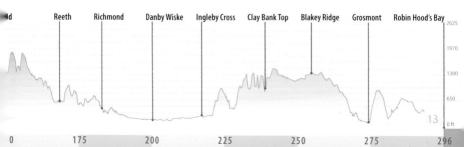

Fitness and preparation

If you haven't done much walking before, we strongly advise that you tackle the walk with someone who is experienced, especially in the use of a map and compass. Well before your departure date, do several consecutive all-day walks involving uphill work, to test your footwear and to build up fitness. Better still, do a long-distance walk of 'only' 3-5 days. Carry a medium-weight daypack to become accustomed to walking with a load. There's no avoiding long ascents and descents, especially in the Lake District.

Experienced long-distance walkers consider this route more challenging than most of the popular National Trails in England and Wales and Scotland's West Highland Way. It's definitely not the ideal choice for your first long-distance walk, though splitting it into 2-3 separate walks makes it more feasible. For advice on choosing and buying gear, obtain our *Notes for novices*: see page 111.

Travel planning

The nearest airport to the walk is Manchester, for flights from North America, western Europe, and elsewhere in the British Isles. Train services link to St Bees via Barrow-in-Furness and to York: see also the foot of page 11 for minibus transfer options.

To St Bees

Virgin Trains run a service between London Euston and Glasgow via Carlisle: change there for Northern Rail trains to St Bees. Coach travel with National Express is less expensive but requires you to change at Carlisle and Whitehaven to Stagecoach Northwest local buses.

From Robin Hood's Bay

Robin Hood's Bay is not on a railway line. Take a bus to Scarborough for a Transpennine Express train to York and onward connections with National Express East Coast to London and the north. Alternatively, go by bus to Whitby for coaches to London.

Driving is practicable only if you have a non-walking member of your party, or are using a baggage transfer service which provides parking at their base.

Intermediate services

If you are planning to do the walk in two or more separate trips, intermediate train and bus services are vital. Kirkby Stephen (Section 6) is on the Carlisle-Leeds line (run by Northern Rail); connect at Leeds for London, and at Carlisle for the north. Arriva Northeast buses run between Richmond (Section 9) and Darlington.

Glaisdale & Grosmont (Section 14) are on the Whitby-Middlesbrough line, run by Northern Rail. Connect at Middlesbrough for Darlington and National Express East Coast trains to London and the north.

Stagecoach Northwest runs services within the Lake District, and the Little Red Bus goes between Keld (Section 7) and Richmond via Muker (Section 8) and Reeth (Section 8). Contact details of transport providers and online booking services are given on page 110.

Responsible walking

Access

The Countryside and Rights of Way Act 2000 entitles people to walk freely across 'access land' – away from paths – in the mountains, moors, heath and downlands, and in large areas of Forestry Commission ground. Of greater relevance to this walk, which follows defined paths (and tracks and roads), are rights of way – paths which are open to walkers even if the surrounding land is not necessarily access land. Between Orton and Kirkby Stephen in particular (Section 6), you will see signs showing areas of Open Access Land and recommended walking routes (including the Coast to Coast).

Access to paths which are not recognised rights of way is usually governed by agreements, often hard-won, with landowners, so it is vitally important that you keep to the route described. This is particularly important in the Vale of Mowbray between Richmond and Ingleby Cross (Sections 10 and 11), where the route follows a long chain of intricate twists and turns. Wherever you are, the Countryside Code is your guide to responsible walking.

> ### Countryside Code
>
> **Know the Code before you go. Enjoy the outdoors – responsibly.**
>
> **Everyone has the right to be on access land in England and to follow rights of way.**
>
> **Your access rights and responsibilities are explained fully in the Countryside Code.**
>
> **The key points are:**
>
> ✓ **Be safe – plan ahead and follow any signs**
>
> ✓ **Leave gates and property as you find them**
>
> ✓ **Protect plants and animals, and take your litter home**
>
> ✓ **Keep dogs under close control**
>
> ✓ **Consider other people**
>
> **The full Code is available from the Open Access Contact Centre: see page 111.**

Carlton Moor Gliding Club notice

Toilets

Use public toilets wherever possible; those that were open in mid-2009 are shown on the maps and indicated in the Facilities table: see page 7.

If you're caught short in between, the best advice is:

- Choose a discreet spot at least 50 m from paths and buildings, preferably further, and as far as possible from any water course.
- Bury waste in a deep hole: use a plastic trowel, or improvise with boots or poles, and cover the hole with any earth and plant material available.

Dogs

Responsible owners are entitled to take their dogs on this walk. However, think carefully before making this decision. Dogs will be most unwelcome during the lambing season – March to May or June. At any time dogs must, by English law, be kept on a short lead (less than 2 m) near farm animals, and between 1 March and 31 July in most areas of open country.

This is not only to avoid stress to livestock and wildlife, but also for your own and your pet's safety. When walking with your dog on the lead, we strongly advise against entering any fields where cattle are grazing: both you and your dog may be endangered. On public paths, dogs must be kept under close control.

Consider the following:

• Stiles are common along the route and your dog will need to be helped over. This can be strenuous and/or difficult, depending on its weight and attitude.
• Many accommodations (especially hostels) do not accept dogs: check carefully before booking.
• You will need to carry a trowel and disposal bags to clear up after your dog if it fouls a defined path.
• Dogs may disturb ground-nesting birds or young mammals, so your dog must be on a short lead during the breeding season (April to July). Signs in moorland areas indicate sensitive areas for breeding species.
• Is your dog fit enough, especially for the days involving lots of uphill work?

If in doubt, obtain the leaflet *You and your dog in the countryside* from the Open Access Contact Centre: see page 111.

Ground-nesting birds are easily disturbed when breeding

Safety and weather

The Coast to Coast walk needs to be taken seriously since it traverses wild moorland and goes over exposed passes and summits up to 780m/2560 ft. Even a minor accident can have major consequences, especially in sparsely settled country, where the nearest help may be far away.

It's safer to walk with at least one other person or in a group. If you decide to go solo, think how you would handle an emergency, remembering that mobile phone coverage is limited or non-existent in the valleys and may be patchy elsewhere.

The weather is a crucial factor, and it is unpredictable year round: on any one day you could walk through conditions typical of all four seasons. Rain is always likely, and it's vital to have the right gear: damp feet can cause serious blisters. Without good waterproofs, the risk of becoming chilled or hypothermic is high. Specific weather forecasts are available for the national parks you walk through: see page 110.

> ### The Mountain Code
> *To report an accident dial 999 and ask for Mountain Rescue*
>
> #### Before you go
> - *Learn to use map and compass*
> - *Learn the mountain distress signals*
> - *Know basic first aid and the symptoms of exposure*
> - *Plan within your abilities*
> - *Do not pollute water*
> - *Choose a climb which will not interfere with others or wait your turn*
>
> #### When you go
> - *Leave details of your route and check in when you arrive*
> - *Take windproofs, waterproofs, first aid kit and survival bag*
> - *Wear suitable boots*
> - *Take relevant map, compass, torch, whistle, food and drink*

Make sure you set out each day with plenty of food and drink. There are shops at or near the beginning and end of almost all sections, but in sections 4, 5, 6, 8, and 13 no refreshments are available during the day and you will have only what you carry. Some accommodation hosts will, with notice, prepare a packed lunch. Elsewhere, the highlights of your walk may include such memorable refreshment stops as Ravenseat Farm, the Lion Inn and Lord Stones café: see pages 93, 98 and below.

During the relatively short stretches of road walking, walk on the right side of the road, so as to face oncoming traffic. Remember that large tractors may use farm tracks and minor roads. Blind bends are common, and minor roads often narrow and hedge-lined. If two vehicles need to pass, retreat to the verge if there is one, and wait until the road is clear. Extra care is needed while walking along and crossing busy main roads.

Water

Sheep are almost everywhere so it would be foolish to drink untreated water from mountain or moorland streams. However, if you use purifying tablets (perhaps adding something to neutralise the flavour, if need be) you can enjoy unlimited supplies. It's essential to maintain your fluid intake during each day's walk – two litres is the bare minimum, more in warm weather. Set out each day with a full water bladder or bottle, and seize every chance to refill it: most pubs and cafés will oblige genuine customers. If you carry bottled water or drinks, use recycling bins wherever possible.

Lord Stones Café, Carlton Bank

Place names

Throughout the walk you'll encounter place names which may be unfamiliar, even mystifying. The following list interprets the most common ones:

barrow	prehistoric burial cairn	gill	stream, rivulet
beck	stream, rivulet, burn	hause	pass, col, saddle
bield	pen, animal shelter	how	knoll, small hill
clough	valley	rigg	ridge
combe	valley	scar	cliff
dale	valley	scaur	tidal rock platform
dub	deep pool, pond	sea fret	sea mist, haar around the east coast
fell	moorland, hill, mountain	tarn	pool on hill or mountain
force, foss	waterfall	tumulus	prehistoric burial mound

Packing checklist

The list is divided into essential and desirable items. Gaiters are valuable for keeping boots and trousers dry and mud-free, and for protection from nettles and bushes where ticks may lurk. If you haven't worn your waterproof trousers recently, test them before you go, when there's still time to re-proof or replace them.

Essential

- rucksack (minimum 35 litres)
- waterproof rucksack cover or liner(s)
- comfortable walking boots
- specialist walking socks
- waterproof jacket and overtrousers
- clothing in layers (tops, trousers, jacket)
- gaiters
- hats for warmth and sun protection
- gloves
- guidebook and compass
- water carrier and plenty of water (or purification tablets)
- food to last between supply points
- whistle and torch
- first aid kit, including blister treatment
- toilet tissue (preferably biodegradable)
- personal toiletries, with towel if hostelling
- insect repellent, sun protection (summer)
- cash (including coins for public phones)
- credit and/or debit cards

Desirable

- walking poles
- spare socks and small towel (for stream crossings)
- plastic bag(s) for litter
- camera
- plenty of spare memory/film for camera
- spare batteries or charger for camera
- binoculars (useful for watching wildlife)
- notebook and pen
- pouch or secure pockets for keeping small items handy and safe
- mobile phone
- survival bag (essential in winter)

For campers

The above list assumes that you are using hostels or B&Bs. If you are camping, you'll also need a tent, sleeping gear, cooking utensils, portable stove, fuel and food, and a much larger rucksack to carry it all.

2·1 Geology and scenery

Below we divide the route into seven sections: west coast, Lake District, Westmorland plateau, Pennines and Yorkshire Dales, Vale of Mowbray, North York Moors, and the east coast. This is an expanded version of Wainwright's own six-fold classification.

West coast

This coast is typified by cliffs up to 100 m high at St Bees Head: see the photographs on pages 30 and 39. These red sandstone and shales were formed about 190 million years ago. The gently undulating plains roll away eastwards towards the Lake District foothills.

Lake District

With the route in mind, the Lake District can be described as a glaciated highland based on volcanic rocks and slates. The line of the walk traverses the outpourings of the Borrowdale volcano, 450 million years ago, notably in the form of granite at the eastern end of Ennerdale.

The slates that are so obvious around Honister Pass are even older, formed from compressed marine sediments. The pass sits on the crux of a classic U-shaped valley – striking evidence of the action of glaciers and meltwater during and after the last Ice Age, about two million years ago.

Westmorland plateau

During the last Ice Age, glaciers scoured the bedrock limestone and eventually a smooth, flat surface emerged. Subsequent weathering and rainwater widened and deepened cracks in the rock, creating patterns of blocks of rock, called *clints*, separated by fissures called *grikes*. These grikes provide a sheltered environment for rare ferns and butterflies.

Limestone pavement (below) and close-up (above)

Generally known as limestone pavement, this feature is of international importance. About one-third of Britain's limestone pavement is found in these westerly regions of the plateau, which extends from near Shap to the Eden valley in which Kirkby Stephen stands. You may also see a few outcrops on the lower reaches of the Pennines, for example on the green route down to the B6270.

Glacial erratic: see page 58

Granite boulders known as *erratics* are relics of glacial retreat at the end of the last Ice Age. There are fine examples sitting on flat limestone slabs close to the 64-mile mark. They were carried from their original home by vast masses of ice, then left behind after the thaw.

Pennines and Yorkshire Dales

The main underlying rock in this area is limestone which, with outcrops of shale and sandstone, is overlaid by millstone grit, a coarse sedimentary rock akin to sandstone. Swaledale, the dominant feature of the walk here, is a glaciated valley, like many of the Yorkshire dales. In this section, you reach the Pennine watershed near Nine Standards: to the west, streams drain into the Irish Sea, whereas to the east they drain to the North Sea.

Vale of Mowbray

The vale has the subtlest profile of any section of the walk, with very few significant hills, and includes Danby Wiske, the lowest inland point on the walk at a mere 35 m/115 ft. The gently undulating, fertile farmland rests on a mix of sand, gravel and glacial deposits, left behind as ice sheets receded at the end of the last Ice Age.

Low-lying fields near Danby Wiske

North York Moors

The North York Moors form an undulating plateau, its spine running west-east, with Urra Moor its highest point (454 m/1490 ft). The southern slopes are gentle, whereas the north-facing escarpment is steep and craggy. The route follows the ridge which is made of sandstone, with bands of shale and ironstone outcropping along its northern slope. During the last Ice Age, the highest ground was ice-free, overlooking glaciers in the valleys and the plains below.

East coast

Fringing a narrow coastal plain, the shale and limestone of the high sea cliffs are topped by sandstone. Robin Hood's Bay is one of the best sites in Britain for finding fossils, marine life trapped in mud millions of years ago. The rock platforms, known as *scaurs* and exposed at low tide, consist of limestone and blue shale.

Scaurs below the cliffs near Robin Hood's Bay

North York Moors

2·2 National parks in England & Wales

William Wordsworth was far ahead of his time when he declared early in the 19th century that the Lake District was 'a sort of national property, in which every man has a right and interest who has an eye to perceive and a heart to enjoy'. During the early 20th century, outdoors organisations, including those representing walkers, became increasingly vociferous and active in their demands for greater access to the countryside. In 1931 a government inquiry recommended that a National Parks Authority be set up to select areas to be designated as national parks.

An important catalyst was the mass trespass on Kinder Scout in the Peak District in April 1932, after which five ramblers were arrested and imprisoned. This united the ramblers' cause. Not only were people determined to achieve greater access to mountain and moorland, but popular momentum for the creation of national parks also grew.

Undaunted, campaigners including the Youth Hostels Association and the Ramblers Association joined forces in a Standing Committee on National Parks in 1935. They lobbied the government to protect and improve access to the countryside. World War 2 intervened, but happily the Labour Party's plans for post-war reconstruction led to the publication in 1945 of a White Paper on National Parks by planner John Dower.

Four years later, the *National Parks and Access to the Countryside Act* provided for their creation. The Peak District was first, set up in 1951, and by 1960 there were 10 in England and Wales. The number now stands at 12, with two in Scotland.

Independent National Park Authorities aim to achieve two goals:
• to conserve and enhance the natural beauty and wildlife and cultural heritage of the national parks
• to promote opportunities for the public understanding and enjoyment of the special qualities of the parks.
Park authorities also have a duty to foster the economic and social wellbeing of local communities within the parks.

The parks are not national property, as in many new world countries. They are owned by the people who live and work in them, and towns and villages, roads and other signs of human activity are part of the manmade landscape. Visitors need to remember that Britain has a comparatively high population density and that large tracts of unsettled land simply don't exist. In response to this reality, the parks' goals include protection of the farms, villages and towns within the parks' boundaries.

More than half of the C2C route lies within three national parks described on page 24. To find out more, go to each park's website or read further: see pages 110 and 111.

Over Swaledale in the Yorkshire Dales

Created in 1951, the **Lake District National Park** is one of the earliest in England, and it's by far the largest. You enter the park along Nannycatch Beck, en route to Ennerdale Bridge, and exit at Shap Abbey, about 50 miles (80 km) further east. Not all of its statistics are enviable: Seatoller, in the heart of the park, is England's wettest inhabited place, enduring 140 in (3550 mm) of rain each year.

The park's dominant features are its high ridges and peaks, crowned by Scafell Pike, the highest peak in England at 978 m/3209 ft, and its many fine lakes (or meres). Equally important is the park's wonderfully varied landscape: complex geological structure, diverse woodlands, intricate mosaic of farmland and distinctive slate buildings. Above all, it has a wonderful range of wildlife.

Almost 59% of the park is privately owned, a comparatively low proportion among English NPs, and about 25% belongs to the National Trust. The park's population of about 42,400 is swollen by enormous numbers of visitors – 15.2 million annually. Fortunately this number seems hard to believe when you're enjoying the comparative isolation of Angle Tarn.

The **Yorkshire Dales National Park** was established in 1954. You enter it about half a mile south of Nine Standards (see page 64-5), and cross its eastern boundary near West Applegarth, *en route* to Richmond. Its outstanding feature is the diversity of its dales: the very beautiful Swaledale dominates the route for a couple of days. Even so, moorlands comprise more than half the park's area, with a similar area of farmland, whilst woodlands, confined to the shelter of the dales, are relatively limited.

The park's diverse cultural heritage ranges from the extensive remains of mining to the distinctive stone barns dotted along the hillsides. It's home to about 20,000 people, but still manages to absorb 12.6 million visitors per year, more in the southern reaches than in the quieter north, through which the C2C passes. Some 96% of the park is privately owned, the highest proportion among the English parks.

The **North York Moors National Park** extends eastwards from Ingleby Cross to the North Sea. Created in 1952, it has a great variety of landscapes and many historic sites. It includes the largest continuous area of heather moorland in England, sheltered valleys, broadleaved woodlands, coastal cliffs, harbours, rivers, farmland, and it hosts a wealth of wildlife.

The North York Moors is also rich in ancient archaeological sites, religious monuments and the remains of historic mining activity. The short coastline along which the C2C runs is only a small part of the 26 miles (42 km) of coast protected by the park. Much of it is of modest altitude, its highest point being merely 454 m (1490 ft) at Round Hill on Urra Moor. With a population of about 25,000, the park is less frequented by visitors than the Lakes or Dales, a mere 9 million annually. About 80% of the land in the park is privately owned.

2·3 Alfred Wainwright

Nobody has influenced walking in the Lake District more than Alfred Wainwright (1907-1991). Nor has any individual created a more popular walk anywhere in the British Isles.

Having grown up in Blackburn, Lancashire, AW made a career in local government, retiring from Kendal Borough Council as borough treasurer in the late 1960s. He first visited the Lake District in 1930 and was sufficiently smitten to return occasionally. His move to Kendal in 1940 gave him the opportunity to go walking every weekend. From the outset he kept diaries and made sketches of his walks.

By 1952 the shortcomings of official maps impelled him to begin work on his own, hand-drawn maps, based on meticulous observation during his solo walks. The first guidebook, published in 1955, was paid for by Wainwright himself. *The Westmorland Gazette* soon took on the role of printer and publisher of his unique, pocket-sized books, complete with hand drawn maps and text. His seven *Pictorial Guides to the Lakeland Fells* became an essential item in every walker's pack.

He walked the Pennine Way in 1967, and a guidebook followed, even though his experience had scarcely been enjoyable. However, it inspired him to devise his own long-distance walk, which he described as 'a harmless and enjoyable walk across England.' He famously concluded his book: 'I finished the Pennine Way with relief, the Coast to Coast Walk with regret. That's the difference.'

After diligent research at home poring over maps, and much work on the ground, trying to find long-neglected rights of way, the guide to his Coast to Coast walk was published in 1973. He readily admitted that it was his pride and joy. For the rest of his life, he was the somewhat reluctant focus of a one-man media spotlight based on his prodigious output of books, with many radio and TV appearances.

In accordance with his wishes, his ashes were scattered on his beloved Hay Stacks, on the ridge above Black Sail Youth Hostel: see page 47.

Despite his gruff public persona, he was an incomparable author, artist and champion of the outdoors, and of the Lake District in particular.

2·4 Prehistory and history

Prehistory

Although people have lived for thousands of years throughout most of the area through which the C2C passes, there is little substantial evidence of their presence. It needs a practised eye and low light to identify some features marked on the map (for example the earthwork at mile 58 just west of Shap) and, in the case of features in cultivated fields, the absence of long grass or crops. In many cases, we have to accept archaeologists' expertise in identifying the evidence. An example of this is the exploitation of iron ore in Rosedale, which may have begun during the Iron Age, about 700 BC to 500 AD.

During the Iron Age, woodlands were cleared, and new crops and farming techniques developed. As a result extensive patterns of enclosed fields were developed. Perhaps the most obvious prehistoric feature is Severals Iron Age settlement above Smardale between Orton and Kirkby Stephen: see page 62. On a sloping site, it's easier to see the stone outlines of enclosures, circular and more angular structures, and the ridges and furrows of cultivation terraces. It's best viewed from the south, early in the morning or evening, when shadows are long.

You may wish to visit other sites within easy reach of the route. One example is Oddendale stone circle, just west of the route between miles 62 and 63. Dating from the Bronze Age (about 2100 BC to 700 BC), it consists of two concentric low-lying circles of limestone. The outer ring is about 85 feet in diameter, with 32 stones, and the inner cairn circle is kerbed with a diameter of about 25 feet. Another could be Croglam Hill Fort, at mile 81 close to Kirkby Stephen. This Iron Age fort comprises a shallow ditch and low outer bank enclosing the summit of a small oval hill.

History

The countryside, villages and small towns through which you walk are rich in features marking out a long and varied history of human settlement. Among the oldest are some fine religious establishments. Marrick Priory has a prominent 12th century tower, but is now used as an outdoor centre: see page 76. St Bees Priory Church, with its marvellous west doorway, also dates back to the 12th century: see page 38. Shap Abbey was built during the 12th and 13th centuries: see page 56.

Tower of Marrick Priory

Of them all, Mount Grace Priory is the most substantial. This is England's best preserved Charterhouse, and well worth a visit if your schedule allows: see panel and photograph below.

The historic town of Richmond makes a splendid interlude, with its magnificent 11th century castle, cobbled market place, and Georgian town buildings: see pages 80-1. Keld's name derives from the Norse language, whilst Kirkby Stephen was granted a charter in the 14th century, after the establishment of its Cathedral of the Dales: see page 63.

People have moved about on foot or horseback from time immemorial. From early Christian times, guidestones, crosses and boundary markers were erected on the featureless vastness of the moors: see page 101. Other ancient routes include the pony track used to move coal from Glaisdale Moor down into Great Fryup Dale, and the old trade route through Last Arncliffe Wood. For centuries, cattle were driven cross-country along well-used routes to markets in the south, with Orton and Kirkby Stephen important staging points. Smardale Bridge, between the two, was right on this drove road.

i **Mount Grace Priory**
Only 1 km off-route (leave at Park House, see page 92, 2nd bullet), this priory was founded in 1398. Unlike most monks who took meals and worshipped together, Carthusians lived as hermits, even having meals passed into their cells. The reconstructed Cell 8 lets you see the austere furnishings and separate garden. You enter through the Lascelles Manor House (1654), rebuilt in about 1900 as an Arts & Crafts country house by Sir Lowthian Bell, a rich industrialist. It's open Thursday to Monday 10.00-18.00 in summer; Thursday-Sunday 10.00-16.00, from November to March inclusive. Small admission charge, tel 01609 883494.

Mount Grace Priory

Railways arrived in the mid-19th century and spread widely across the north of England, but many were closed in the 20th. You may have used a survivor – Cumbria's coastal route – to reach St Bees by train. The Settle-Carlisle line, near Kirkby Stephen, was saved from closure in 1989. A tribute to the popular love of railways is the preserved North York Moors steam railway. The route passes through Grosmont, its terminus: see page 102.

The route has fleeting encounters with other disused lines, including the Whitehaven-Cleator-Egremont line, now a cycle path, and the Scarborough-Whitby line, between High Hawsker and the coast. Near Smardale Bridge you can see the magnificent Smardale Gill viaduct: see below and page 62. Built in 1861 by Sir Thomas Bouch to carry coke from the eastern coalfields to the furnaces of Cumberland, it has 14 arches and stands 90 feet high. The line was closed in 1962, but a group of enthusiasts saved it from demolition in the late 1980s, and it now carries a permissive footpath through Smardale Gill nature reserve.

Throughout the walk, mining pre-dates the railways. All but one of the mines are now merely landscape features, the remarkable exception being England's only working slate mine at Honister Pass: see page 47. Its greenish Westmorland slate is highly prized, with the best quality exported and used to roof notable buildings. Much slate appears in local buildings, especially in Borrowdale.

Slate may have been quarried here since Roman times, and slate roofing is seen in many 13th century monastic buildings. Production here was recorded by William Wordsworth in his diaries. In 1833, mines were opened, output increased and a tramway was built: see page 46, 8th bullet. Later, transport improved with roads and an aerial ropeway (1928) to carry the slate to Honister Pass for cutting and finishing. Factory workers, who lived on-site during the week in what is now Honister Hause Youth Hostel, returned home at weekends.

Smardale Gill old viaduct

The history of lead mining in Swaledale also dates back to Roman times, perhaps even to the Bronze Age. Early extraction was mainly by 'hushing': dams were built across streams then breached to release great surges of water that scoured the hillsides, exposing veins of lead. Output increased dramatically from the late 18th century as mining was commercialised, and peaked by about 1840. Decline was gradual through the 19th century, with operations at the Old Gang site surviving the longest. The Old Gang Lead Mining Company was wound up in 1906.

The rich iron ore had been won at the cost of many lives of men, women and children. Mines were unsafe, methods primitive and the smelting mills unhygienic and polluting. Fortunately some of the mining companies enabled their workers to spend time away from the mine. The network of paths, some followed by the C2C, is the welcome legacy. The peat store at Blakethwaite, the Old Gang smelt mill complex and the 18th century Surrender Bridge are scheduled ancient monuments in the care of English Heritage, and legally protected.

Abandoned machinery near Old Gang

Other mining left less obvious traces. Cleator thrived during the 19th century when iron ore and coal were mined locally, and Glaisdale and Grosmont were also iron ore boom villages. Jet (black fossilised wood) was extracted from the North York Moors between Carlton Bank and Hasty Bank, and in Scugdale. Near Littlebeck and elsewhere alum was taken from frost-resistant clay and used for fixing dyes in textiles. It was overtaken by the development of chemical dyes after the 1870s. On a smaller scale, locally abundant limestone was burned in kilns to produce fertiliser. There's a fine limekiln beside the path just after you cross the B6260 road, under a mile north of Orton: see page 58.

Old Gang smelt mill

2·5   Habitats and wildlife

The Coast to Coast walk passes through a range of habitats, described below:
- coast
- moorland
- woodland and hedgerows
- grassland and farmland

Birds and mammals are more active at the beginning and end of the day, so you're more likely to see them if you start very early or go for a stroll in the evening. Midges also follow this pattern, so between May and September cover up and apply repellent. Don't forget binoculars, if you have them.

Coast

At St Bees Head, a nature reserve hosts the largest seabird colony in north-west England, cared for by the Royal Society for the Protection of Birds. During the nesting season, every available ledge on the near-vertical cliffs is occupied, the air filled with the cries of seabirds arriving and departing. Sleek dark-headed guillemots perch upright on their rock ledge and keep up a loud growling call. The kittiwake is a small gull-like bird, with black wing tips, black legs and yellow bill. Its call is a trademark *kitti-waake*.

Cormorants frequent South Head, best seen when they're perching on rocks or posts, with their wings spread out to dry. At a distance they appear almost uniformly black. The dense shrubs close to the cliff edge shelter various small birds. The whitethroat lives up to its name with white throat, grey head and red-brown wings, though it's shy and hard to spot. The male stonechat has a dark brown head with white neck patches, and chestnut underparts, and it favours gorse bushes. The linnet has a distinctive red crown patch on its grey head, and a red chest.

Just inland, as well as in upland areas, all-black ravens are a common sight, performing aerial acrobatics, or soaring and gliding at great height. You may spot an occasional peregrine – incredibly fast on the wing in pursuit of prey, it has a blue-grey back, wings and head.

Seabirds nesting near St Bees Head

Thrift or sea pink is perhaps the most common wildflower, and one of the hardiest, making splashes of pink or mauve on exposed clifftops and rocky places from spring until midsummer. Sea campion has an odd-looking white flower, its petals sprouting from a bulbous tube, and its leaves are lance-shaped. Dense, spiny bushes of flowering gorse are common along the coast, as well as inland. From early spring, you'll see their yellow flowers and smell their almond perfume: see the photograph on page 37.

Thrift flourishes in rocky niches

The east coast cliffs are much less suitable for nesting, though you will see herring gulls, and perhaps some cormorants and fulmars. The rock platforms and sandy shores are ideal for foraging oystercatchers: they are easy to identify by their black head with long red-orange bill, black chest and back with white underparts, and their trademark – a loud, persistent *pik-pik* call.

The curlew is Europe's largest wading bird, often seen on rocks at low tide, and in estuaries. Its long curved bill is distinctive, and its patterned plumage makes for good camouflage. This helps in the breeding season (spring), when they nest on the moors.

Curlew breed on the moors

Moorland

The moors are
carpeted with hardy
heather, in flower from
midsummer. There are two kinds:
bell has larger, deep purple flowers, whereas
ling is pinker. Both have tough, twisted stems and tiny
needle-shaped leaves. Traditionally, these made excellent
roofing material. Flowers were put to good use in dyeing, and in
brewing, a tradition maintained to this day.

The golden plover has a plaintive whistle, evoking the remoteness
of its native moors. It often stands watch on a low rock, and its flight is low and
unswerving. Its mottled golden brown upper parts blend well with its surroundings,
making it easier to hear than to see. In summer it favours moorland, whilst in winter it
moves to lowland fields, often forming large flocks with lapwings.

In many places, heather moorlands are now managed for game shooting. During
April each year, selected strips are burnt to encourage new growth and seed
germination, to provide food and a patchwork habitat for game birds, including
pheasant and grouse. Shooting butts (shelters) are used during the season, which
runs from 12 August to 10 December. Shooting is an important component of the
local economy, and you'll see butts on the route, particularly on the descent to
Ravenseat: see page 69.

Pheasant are larger than grouse, and the male's long tail and dark green head with
red wattles is distinctive. Like grouse, they erupt in a whirr of rapid wing beats and
raucous cackling when startled. Red grouse have a plump body and short tail, and
are highly prized as game birds. The male is dark brown with distinctive red eye
patches, whereas the female is mottled and well camouflaged.

Red grouse (male) in heather

During early summer the lapwing performs aerial acrobatics – dipping, twisting and rolling. On the ground it's easily identified by the wispy crest on its black head, and very dark back. It frequents the moorland mainly during summer, and may also be seen in farmland and along the coast.

Red deer stag

A bird of almost iconic status for this route is the skylark. It pours out its wistful song as it ascends ever higher, out of sight, seeming to herald better weather. It's a small streaky brown bird with a crest, easier to spot in display flight than when at rest. It forages for seeds and insects: see also page 37.

Mammals are comparatively scarce, but you may be lucky enough to see red deer: keep a lookout on the climb out of Patterdale. The stag presents a fine silhouette with its branching, pointed antlers and bright red-brown summer coat. The hind is much smaller and lacks antlers.

Sheep are everywhere. They are valuable in helping to maintain the open, low vegetation that many other species need to survive. Two local breeds are worth singling out: Swaledales in the Dales and Herdwicks in the Lake District. Swaledales have a black face, white muzzle and white wool. Herdwicks are particularly hardy, and have white head and legs. In the ewes, their blackish wool tends to turn grey-blue with age.

Hardy Herdwick sheep

Woodland and hedgerows

Woodlands are scattered widely throughout the walk and provide welcome shelter from open moorland. There's a wide range of tree species along the route. Sessile and English oaks are among the largest and oldest. Although their leaves are similar – with characteristic deep lobes – they can be distinguished by their acorns. Those on the sessile oak almost 'sit' on the leaves, whereas on the English oak they hang from obvious stalks (or *peduncles*).

Wood anemone

Stately, spreading beech trees flourish best on limestone. They have smooth bark and dark green and glossy leaves that turn a magnificent russet during autumn. The hardy birch is usually found on moorland edges, and has smooth, silvery bark, which becomes furrowed and rough in mature trees. Its pointed leaves turn yellow-brown in autumn.

Autumn is the time when trees become a food source. Clusters of nuts appear on the hazel – a smallish, rather untidy tree with rounded, serrated leaves. Hazelnuts are a favourite of the red squirrel. The spiny-leaved holly produces its trademark red berries long before Christmas. The grey-barked rowan has leaves growing in pairs along the stem. From late summer, its thick clusters of red berries offer a fine food source: see below.

Among the many wildflowers that you may see in woodland, three stand out. Bluebells have delicate bell-shaped flowers on a slender stem. Wild primrose has crinkly, rounded leaves and yellow flowers in spring. The wood anemone grows prolifically during spring, its white flowers easily shaken by the wind. Hence it is named after *anemos*, the Greek wind god: see photograph above.

Rowan tree with autumn berries

Woodlands provide food, shelter and nesting sites for a variety of smaller birds including treecreepers and blue tits. The treecreeper has variegated brown and gold plumage, providing good camouflage. Its slender curved bill digs into tree bark while its stiff pointed tail provides support against the trunk. The blue tit has a prominent yellow chest, black eye strip, with blue only on its head, outer wings and tail

The buzzard, probably the most common bird of prey along the route, frequents woodlands and is often also seen perched on a fence post, or wheeling and gliding while hunting for prey. Its back and wings

Red squirrel with nesting material in her mouth

are mottled and patterned brown, with some white beneath. Then there's the unforgettable springtime visitor, the cuckoo. Despite the persistence of its call, it's very difficult to catch sight of this undistinguished greyish bird.

The route passes though a few conifer plantations, notably in Ennerdale. Dominated by Sitka spruce and lodgepole pine, they are comparatively poor in wildlife, with a few exceptions, notably the red squirrel. Very much at home in conifer forests, its coat is more chestnut brown than red, and the long bushy tail a much lighter shade. It is smaller than its grey American cousin, and its survival is threatened by the squirrelpox disease carried by the grey. Squirrels strip the scales from ripe pine cones to uncover the seeds, then discard the chewed cone, a sure sign of their presence.

Buzzard feeding on rabbit

Hedgerows, often regarded as an endangered feature of the English countryside, are alive and thriving along the route, particularly between Bolton-on-Swale and Ingleby Cross. These dense rows of bushes between fields may include hawthorn, with pinkish white flowers and masses of thorns; blackthorn, with blue-black fruit, narrow leaves and abundant white flowers in early spring; pink and white-flowering dog rose; and bramble, a wonderful source of free food during late summer and autumn.

Small Tortoiseshell

Grassland and farmland

Butterflies are common in grassland wherever their favourite foods – including thistles and nettles – are found. The Small Tortoiseshell has orange wings with dark bands and markings, and a white spot on each wingtip. The colourful Painted Lady is a long-distance migrant from North Africa and beyond. It also has orange wings, but with dark wingtips with white spots and more dark markings near its tail.

In damp areas of unimproved grassland, look out for two insect-eating plants: butterwort and sundew. The butterwort carries small purple flowers on slender long stems. Its pale green leaves are covered with sticky glands which trap and digest small insects. The sundew has small rounded leaves edged with fine hairs which exude a sweet juice that attracts small insects. The hairs then curl over the hapless insect, which is soon digested by the plant.

Sundew

In farmland areas such as Swaledale, there are fine examples of hay meadow. Selected fields are cleared of stock during spring and cut for hay in July or August. Meantime, an abundance of species creates a patchwork of colours, with yellow-flowering birdsfoot trefoil, speedwell, thistles, common ragwort, yarrow, clover, sorrel and meadow buttercup.

The skylark's preferred habitat is farmland, but intensive farming practices have led to a 75% decline in their numbers between 1972 and 1996. They are ground-nesting, and need to produce several broods a year to sustain their population. Once widespread throughout Britain, you are now more likely to see them higher up on the moors.

Bee feeding on a thistle

Skylark perching on gorse

St Bees

It is generally believed that an Irish princess founded St Bega's nunnery as early as the 7th century, though it survived for only 200 years. St Bega is commemorated in a small park beside Station Road.

A few centuries later, the Benedictines founded a priory on the site in 1120. Built of the local red sandstone, it was dissolved during the 16th century then partly restored about a century later, having become the parish church of St Mary and St Bega. More extensive restoration followed in the 19th century. Its most striking original feature is the magnificent

West door, St Bees Priory Church

Normanesque west door. Leaflets describing various aspects of the local history are available inside the church, which is usually open.

The other outstanding historic building in the village is St Bees School, just across the road from the church, and built of the same red sandstone. It was founded in 1583 by the then Archbishop of Canterbury, Edward Grindal, born in St Bees, and began taking pupils a few years later. The original foundation block and school room are still in use in this well-known independent boarding school. Grindal's home, behind the Queens Hotel, is now the oldest standing building in the village.

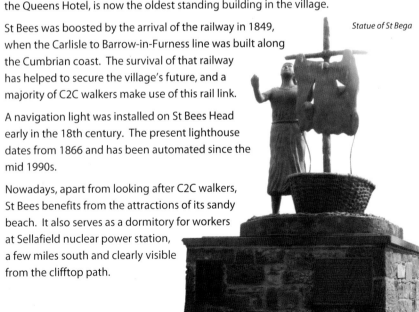

Statue of St Bega

St Bees was boosted by the arrival of the railway in 1849, when the Carlisle to Barrow-in-Furness line was built along the Cumbrian coast. The survival of that railway has helped to secure the village's future, and a majority of C2C walkers make use of this rail link.

A navigation light was installed on St Bees Head early in the 18th century. The present lighthouse dates from 1866 and has been automated since the mid 1990s.

Nowadays, apart from looking after C2C walkers, St Bees benefits from the attractions of its sandy beach. It also serves as a dormitory for workers at Sellafield nuclear power station, a few miles south and clearly visible from the clifftop path.

1 St Bees to Ennerdale Bridge

Distance	14 miles (22.5 km)
Terrain	roadside path, clifftop path, minor roads, tracks and field paths, then more roads and paths, including some roadside
Food and drink	St Bees , Moor Row, Cleator, Ennerdale Bridge
Summary	wonderful scenic start along cliff tops; undulating countryside and quiet villages; inspirational view from Dent, followed by delightful Nannycatch Beck

Each band of colour represents 50 m

St Bees — Sandwith — Cleator — Dent — Ennerdale Bridge

0 km   5   10   15   20

- From St Bees station, cross the railway line and turn left along Station Road, soon passing a statue of St Bega in a small park. Follow the road to the beach car park, bending right.

- Cross the car park to follow a path past toilets and a play area to a large stone-built pillar marking the start. Good luck!

- Bear right beside the caravan park fence and down across a footbridge. A clear path leads uphill, then between a field and the cliff edge. Ignore a path to the right at a junction and continue on the seaward side of the fence.

Toward St Bees Head

- Pass a viewpoint from where both the Isle of Man and the Lake District mountains may be visible. The path, on the landward side of the fence, skirts Fleswick Bay and rises over St Bees Head.

- Along the way, bird observation enclosures are worth the tiny diversions to see the cliffs jam-packed with nests. Beyond a track to St Bees lighthouse and Tarnflatt Hall, the path runs along the edge of cliffs and a landslip.

- At a disused quarry, follow the wide track, then bear left. Turn right at a T-junction and follow this minor road to Sandwith. Turn left at a T-junction, then right beside a pub.

- Go straight on at the crossroads for a short distance then follow a path that bends left, then right. Bear left at houses, through a gate, then right through a farmyard to a track. Cross the B5345 and continue past Bell House and downhill.

- Bear right at a fork and go through a gate. After a bend, swing left down a minor track to a gate, then drop down to a railway underpass. Bear left across the field. On the far side, cross a footbridge to a path.

- Go up to a fence then left to a minor track junction. Bear left to a marker post, then bear right up a rough field path. Ford a small stream; continue up to a stile and go under the old railway track up to a road.

- Cross the A595 to an encouraging C2C statue (only 184 miles to go, it says) and press on through Moor Row. Turn right towards Egremont. After a right bend, pass a track on the left, then turn left along a signposted path.

- Traverse a succession of field paths and stiles, a sliver of a paved cycle track, then bear left to a field path, or an alternative, as indicated. Either way, soon bend right beside a sports field along Wainwright Passage. Continue to the A5086 in Cleator and turn left.

- Turn right along Kiln Brow, then first right. Cross the River Ehen bridge, then follow a track around a sharp left bend up to another left turn at farm buildings.

St Bees lighthouse

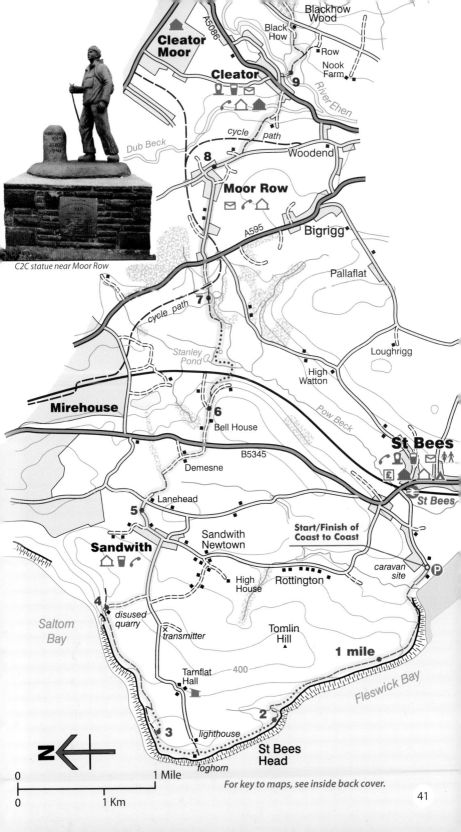

Blackhow Wood

Cleator Moor

A5086

Black How

Row

Nook Farm

Cleator

9

River Ehen

cycle path

Woodend

Dub Beck

8

Moor Row

A595

Bigrigg

Pallaflat

cycle path

7

Stanley Pond

Loughrigg

High Watton

Mirehouse

Pow Beck

6

Bell House

St Bees

B5345

£

Demesne

Lanehead

5

Sandwith Newtown

Start/Finish of Coast to Coast

St Bees

Sandwith

caravan site

P

High House

Rottington

4

Saltom Bay

disused quarry

x transmitter

Tomlin Hill

1 mile

400

Tarnflat Hall

Fleswick Bay

2

3

lighthouse

St Bees Head

foghorn

N

0   1 Mile

0   1 Km

For key to maps, see inside back cover.

C2C statue near Moor Row

41

- Next, turn right up to a road. Cross over and walk up the through the conifer plantation. Bear left at a fork along a minor track which shortly crosses open ground.

- Continue up, over a stile and up to Dent's summit cairn. The wide view embraces both the coastal plain and the Lake District mountains. Cross the undulating grassy plateau along a path, with a low stone wall on the left at first.

- Descend on a track to a T-junction and turn left. At the next junction, bear left. Beyond a tall stile, follow a grassy track across open ground.

- Now steady yourself for an extremely steep descent. Just when your knees have almost had enough, the path bears left well down and leads to a footbridge over Nannycatch Beck. Walk up its lovely little valley, soon entering the Lake District National Park: see page 24.

- Where the path bends left, ignore waymarkers to the right and continue to a gate; turn right up the valley. The unbridged stream crossings may be tricky after heavy rain. Further uphill, merge with a path from the left.

- Continue up to a junction and turn right. Once you reach the minor road, bear left. Almost immediately you'll pass Kinniside stone circle on the right, generally regarded as a fake.

- Just after the 13-mile mark, diverge left along a signposted footpath, which generally parallels the road. Soon you see Ennerdale Water: an information panel identifies many of the hills in view, some overlooking tomorrow's walk.

- Just past two houses on the right, cross the road and continue on the path. At a road junction, cross to join a path parallel to the road. It ends just short of the River Ehen bridge in the village of Ennerdale Bridge.

Ennerdale Water

Beckfoot

Whins

Anglers'
Crag

Croftfoot

16

weir

Crag
Farm
House

P

Croftfoot

15

Moorend

River Ehen

Fellend

**Ennerdale
Bridge**

14

Swinside

13

Swinside
End

Blakeley
Moss

*Kinniside
Stone
Circle*

Scaly Moss

Standing
Stones

Sillathwaite

Lagget

*Meadley
Reservoir*

Nannycatch Beck

Flat Fell

12

High
Waterside

Low
Waterside

Cathow

11

Uldale
Farm

ULDALE

Hazel
Holme

High
Merebeck

▲ Dent
1131 ft

Kirk Beck

N

0
0

1 Mile
1 Km

10

Blackhow
Wood

**Cleator
Moor**

A5086

Black
How

Row

9

Nook Farm

Cleator

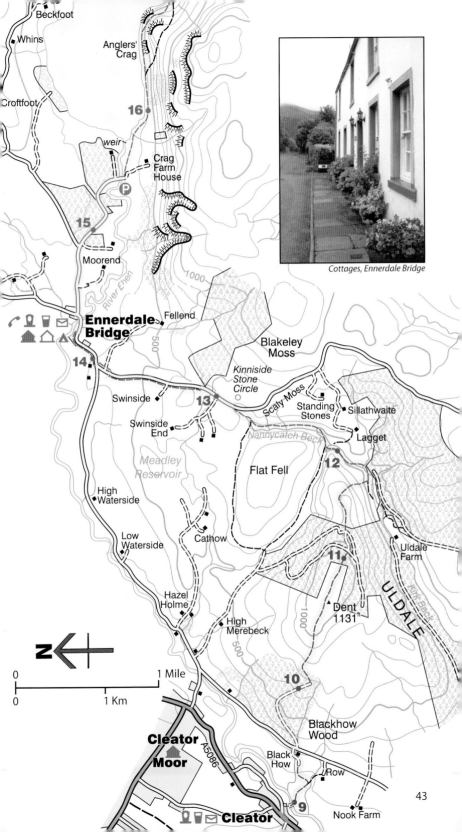

Cottages, Ennerdale Bridge

43

2 Ennerdale Bridge to Rosthwaite

Distance	**16.5 miles (26.5 km)**
Terrain	**quiet road, rocky lakeside path, field paths, forest road. mixture of paths, with one difficult section**
Food and drink	**Ennerdale Bridge, Honister Pass, Seatoller, Rosthwaite**
Summary	**lakeside and mountain paths, with fine views; stark mining landscape, then wooded Borrowdale**

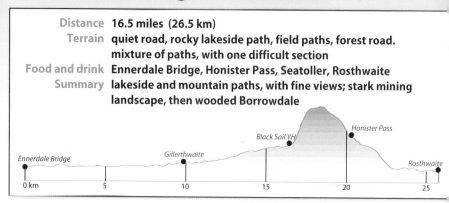

Ennerdale Bridge · Gillerthwaite · Black Sail YH · Honister Pass · Rosthwaite

0 km   5   10   15   20   25

- From the River Ehen bridge, follow the road eastwards. Bear right at the first junction then right again along a road to Ennerdale Water. At the next junction head toward the water.

- Cross a bridge, go past a car park, then left along a track and through a gate. The shoreline path starts near the weir. Pass through a gate into National Trust property.

- Between miles 16 and 17, there's a short high-level alternative path over Anglers' Crag. It involves at least 120 m extra ascent, and its turnoff is obscure, but you may wish to seek it out. If you stay with the main waterside path, take care: it's rocky at first, albeit not treacherous.

- From the eastern shore of Ennerdale Water, continue across grassland. Go through a gate on the right, then bear left with a forest boundary on the right.

- Go through another gate, negotiate a cattle grid and bear left along a track. After about 50 m, bear left over a stile and cross a field to reach a footbridge.

- On the far side, bear right along a path, soon crossing a small stream. Pass Gillerthwaite Field Centre, shortly reaching the forest road which soon passes Ennerdale Youth Hostel.

Waterside path below Anglers Crag

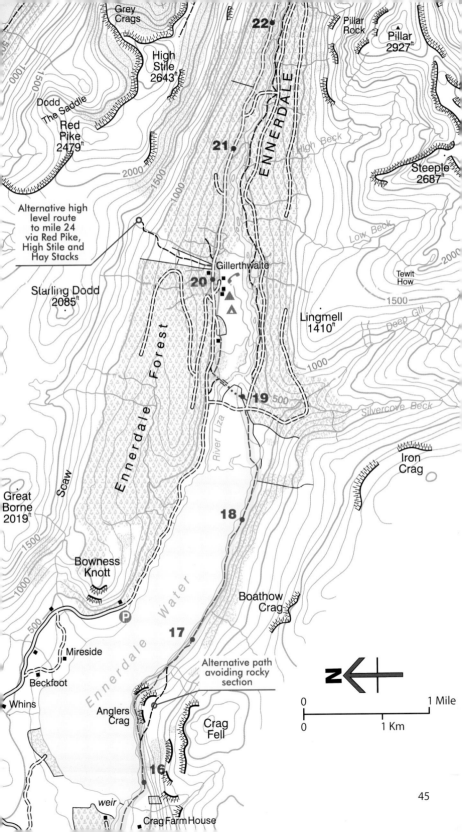

Grey
Crags

22

Pillar
Rock

Pillar
2927ft

High
Stile
2643ft

E
N
N
E
R
D
A
L
E

High Beck

Dodd
The Saddle
Red
Pike
2479ft

21

Steeple
2687

Alternative high
level route
to mile 24
via Red Pike,
High Stile and
Hay Stacks

2000

1500

1000

Low Beck

Gillerthwaite

Tewit
How

20

Starling Dodd
2085ft

Ennerdale Forest

Lingmell
1410ft

1500

Deep Gill

1000

19

500

Silvercove Beck

River Liza

Iron
Crag

Great
Borne
2019ft

Scaw

18

1500

Bowness
Knott

1000

Ennerdale Water

Boathow
Crag

500

P

17

Mireside

Alternative path
avoiding rocky
section

N

Beckfoot

0   1 Mile

Whins

Anglers
Crag

0   1 Km

Crag
Fell

16

weir

Crag Farm House

- From Gillerthwaite, the map shows the start of another alternative path over High Stile and Hay Stacks, rejoining the main route at mile 25.

- The forest road leads up Ennerdale with inspirational views across the tumbling River Liza to the peaks and ridges high above.

- Go through a gate and on to Black Sail Youth Hostel, a former shepherd's hut. It's usually open and drinks are available: use the honesty box. Enjoy its wonderful atmosphere and shelter, for free.

Black Sail Youth Hostel

- From here, do not follow the eroded track that descends right. Instead, walk along the grassy path to its left across the steep slope. It's faint at first, especially across soft spots.

- The path soon becomes clear as it climbs steadily and crosses Loft Beck. It veers left at two large cairns and goes up beside the beck, now with a firm surface.

- Beyond two more crossings, you reach a grassy col from where Ennerdale Water, and Buttermere to the north-west, may be visible.

- A cairned path leads up to a stile then descends gently through the one-time slate mining area, soon with good views of the deep cleft of Honister Pass. The former tramway track is clearly identifiable as a slightly raised path flanked by a stone wall.

- Turn right and descend steeply on the track to Honister Slate Mine with its stockpiles of recently extracted slate, visitor centre and café: see panel opposite.

- Walk down the road to a slight right bend, from where a clear track leads on for a few hundred metres. Then, after a short stretch of path, follow a signposted bridleway, now well away from the road.

- Cross a small stream, go through a gate and about 50 m past some tall conifers, bear right on a path, steeply down to the road. Follow the road through Seatoller.

- Turn left to the car park, following a path to Longthwaite. From its far side, cross a stile and follow a grassy track into Johnny's Wood, soon passing through a gate. Within 25 m, bear right down a stony path.

- Ford a small stream, go through a gate and downhill. After three more gates you're almost at river level. Now for some fun: make your way along ledges in the low cliffs, with a short chain for security, then across small boulders and tree roots.

- Beyond a gate, a broad flat path leads on, past Borrowdale Youth Hostel. Cross the car park, then the bridge on your right.

- Go up and turn left as indicated, across two fields. Pass though a gate to a lane, which bends right, left and right to the main road in Rosthwaite.

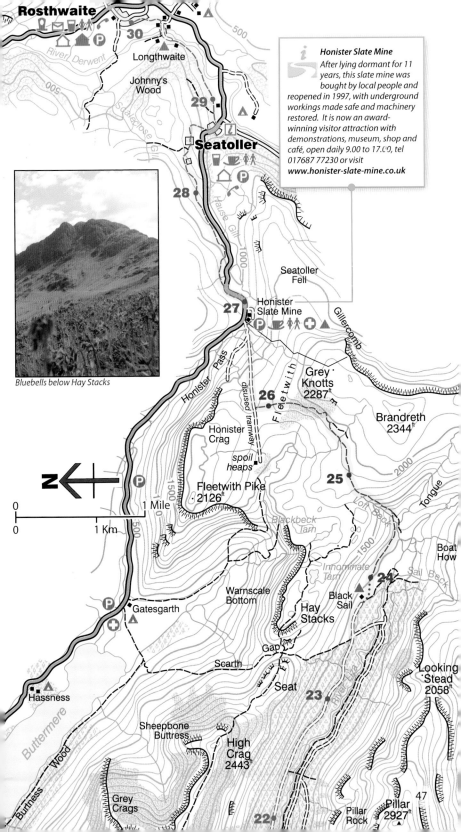

Rosthwaite

River Derwent

Longthwaite

Johnny's Wood

Seatoller Gill

Seatoller

30

29

28

27

26

25

24

23

22

Hause Gill

Honister Pass

Honister Crag

spoil heaps

disused tramway

Fleetwith

Fleetwith Pike
2126ft

Honister Slate Mine

Seatoller Fell

Gillercomb

Grey Knotts
2287ft

Brandreth
2344ft

Tongue

Loft Beck

Blackbeck Tarn

Boat How

Innominate Tarn

Sail Beck

Black Sail

Hay Stacks

Warnscale Bottom

Gatesgarth

Hassness

Buttermere

Bluebells below Hay Stacks

Gap

Scarth

Seat

Looking Stead
2058ft

River Liza

Buttness Wood

Sheepbone Buttress

High Crag
2443ft

Grey Crags

Pillar Rock

Pillar
2927ft

47

N

0 ——— 1 Mile
0 ——— 1 Km

ℹ️ *Honister Slate Mine*
After lying dormant for 11 years, this slate mine was bought by local people and reopened in 1997, with underground workings made safe and machinery restored. It is now an award-winning visitor attraction with demonstrations, museum, shop and café, open daily 9.00 to 17.00, tel 017687 77230 or visit **www.honister-slate-mine.co.uk**

3 Rosthwaite to Patterdale

Distance	**14 miles (22.5 km)**
Terrain	**well-defined but rough, boggy paths; then minor roads, tracks and paths, mostly well-defined**
Food and drink	**Rosthwaite, Grasmere, Patterdale**
Summary	**a challenging day, with two major ascents to 600m/2000ft (can be split at Grasmere); dramatic valleys and wild moorland, then pastoral scenery of Grisedale**

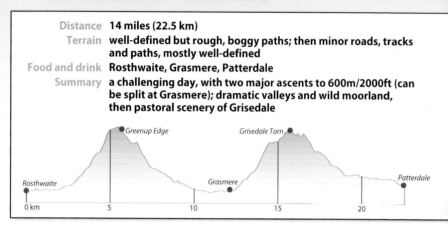

- In Rosthwaite, continue briefly left along the road, then diverge towards Stonethwaite. Cross a bridge and bear right along a path, generally following Greenup Gill.

- From the signposted turnoff to Stonethwaite, continue towards Grasmere. With the valley closing in, cross a footbridge over a tributary of Greenup Gill, below Eagle Crag.

- From a ford over the next tributary, the path steepens and crosses several more streams, some of which could be awkward after heavy rain. Eventually you come to a wide grassy bowl at the foot of a steep climb.

- The lower reach of this stretch isn't clearly defined, so follow the line of cairns. The upper section of the path leads clearly to Lining Crag, an impressive viewpoint.

- Press on up the peaty, rocky slope, again carefully following cairns, to Greenup Edge at the head of Wyth Burn Valley. Descend over boggy ground, surrendering all hope of keeping footwear dry, and negotiating one potentially deep ford.

- From a clearly defined edge at the head of Far Easedale Gill, continue straight down, soon on a clear path. Descend steeply through bog and rocks and across a stream.

South over Grasmere and Dove Lake

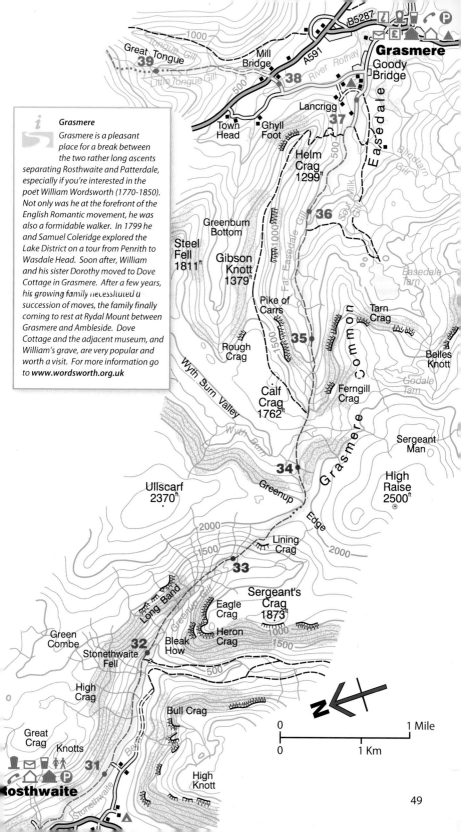

Grasmere

Grasmere is a pleasant place for a break between the two rather long ascents separating Rosthwaite and Patterdale, especially if you're interested in the poet William Wordsworth (1770-1850). Not only was he at the forefront of the English Romantic movement, he was also a formidable walker. In 1799 he and Samuel Coleridge explored the Lake District on a tour from Penrith to Wasdale Head. Soon after, William and his sister Dorothy moved to Dove Cottage in Grasmere. After a few years, his growing family necessitated a succession of moves, the family finally coming to rest at Rydal Mount between Grasmere and Ambleside. Dove Cottage and the adjacent museum, and William's grave, are very popular and worth a visit. For more information go to **www.wordsworth.org.uk**

B5287

Grasmere

Goody Bridge

Mill Bridge

A591

River Rothay

39

Great Tongue

Tongue Gill

Little Tongue Gill

38

37

Lancrigg

Town Head

Ghyll Foot

Helm Crag 1299ft

Sour Milk Gill

Easedale

36

Greenburn Bottom

Steel Fell 1811ft

Gibson Knott 1379ft

Far Easedale Gill

Easedale Tarn

Blindtarn Gill

Pike of Carrs

Tarn Crag

Belles Knott

Rough Crag

35

Ferngill Crag

Godale Tarn

Wyth Burn Valley

Calf Crag 1762ft

Grasmere Common

Sergeant Man

Wyth Burn

34

High Raise 2500ft

Ullscarf 2370ft

Greenup Edge

2000

2000

1500

Lining Crag

1500

33

Sergeant's Crag 1873ft

Long Band

Greenup Gill

Eagle Crag

Heron Crag

1500

Green Combe

Bleak How

32

Stonethwaite Fell

High Crag

500

N

Great Crag

Knotts

Bull Crag

0   1 Mile

0   1 Km

31

High Knott

Rosthwaite

Stonethwaite Beck

- The path gradually improves, but not until you're well down. Cross a bridge; about 50 m past a junction with the Helm Crag path on the left, continue along a road. Turn left along a road signposted to Thorney How Youth Hostel.

- To reach Grasmere, continue for about 100 m, then diverge right along a path. Turn left at its end to reach the village: see panel on page 49.

- For Patterdale, follow the road past the youth hostel; bear right at a junction and up to the A591. Cross directly, with great care, to a track to Patterdale.

- It soon becomes an excellent path ascending beside Tongue Gill. Go through a gate and over a footbridge across a tributary. Ignore a bridge across the main stream.

- The delightfully grassy path leads on, bending right well up, and soon crosses a grassy bowl valley. The final ascent, overlooked by a cluster of crags, is steep and rocky, to a stone wall, above Grisedale Tarn.

- Traverse above the south-eastern shore, ford the outlet stream and continue below the steep slopes of Helvellyn, one of the Lake District's iconic summits at 950m/3118ft. The rocky path drops down past Ruthwaite Lodge (closed).

- At a fork with a footbridge on the left, bear right and go down to a wider bridge. A few hundred metres further on, the track improves, passing beside enclosed woodland.

- The route continues along a road from the Braestead turnoff. Pass a path to Patterdale, then a private road on the left. Diverge right along a public footpath further on.

- A short distance along the fence on the right, cross a stile and continue along generally beside the fence. After about 300 m, descend to cross a stream.

- A wide path leads up, then across, rocky ground with good views of Ullswater. Go through a gate and generally down into woodland.

- Bear right within a few metres to a wide path. Opposite a slate building, bear right and follow a track down to the A592 into Patterdale.

North over Patterdale and Glenridding

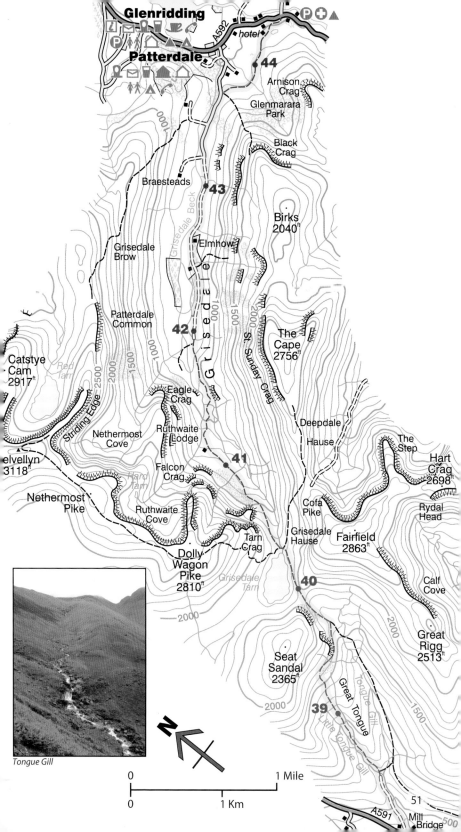

Glenridding

Patterdale

● 44

Arnison Crag

Glenmarara Park

Black Crag

Braesteads ● 43

Birks 2040ft

Grisedale Brow

Elmhow

Patterdale Common

● 42

Catstye Cam 2917ft

The Cape 2756ft

Red Tarn

St Sunday Crag

Striding Edge

Eagle Crag

Nethermost Cove

Ruthwaite Lodge

Deepdale Hause

The Step

elvellyn 3118ft

Falcon Crag

● 41

Hart Crag 2698ft

Nethermost Pike

Hard Tarn

Ruthwaite Cove

Cofa Pike

Rydal Head

Tarn Crag

Grisedale Hause

Fairfield 2863ft

Calf Cove

Dolly Wagon Pike 2810ft

Grisedale Tarn

● 40

Seat Sandal 2365ft

Great Rigg 2513ft

Great Tongue

Little Tongue Gill

Tongue Gill

N

● 39

0		1 Mile
0		1 Km

51

A591

Mill Bridge

4 Patterdale to Shap

Distance	**15½ miles (24.9 km)**
Terrain	**careful route-finding needed from Boredale Hause to Angle Tarn, good paths beside reservoir, then mainly field paths to Shap**
Food and drink	**none between Patterdale and Shap**
Summary	**a day of great contrasts, from Angle Tarn to Kidsty Pike; fine woodlands and rural views, then a historic abbey**

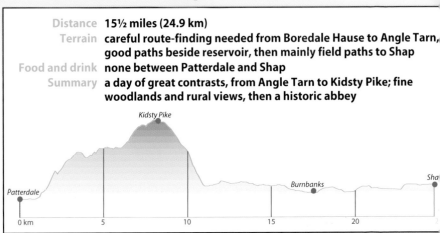

- From Patterdale, almost opposite the track at the main road, follow the minor road leading north-east and crossing Goldrill Beck. At a fork, head for Boredale Hause.

- At the next junction, bear right through a gate towards Boredale and Angle Tarn. Shortly it's right again; pass another path on right and climb past a well-preserved bench commemorating Queen Victoria's diamond jubilee in 1897.

- Continue up to Boredale Hause, a rather boggy col. At the path junction with a cairn, bear right uphill, across a grassy slope.

- Then pass through a narrow defile on a well made path, past a large cairn. Around here are good views of Brotherswater, below to the south-west.

- At a junction, bear right on a good path contouring the slope. Soon Angle Tarn comes into view. The path leads on above the tarn, up a long green valley.

Angle Tarn

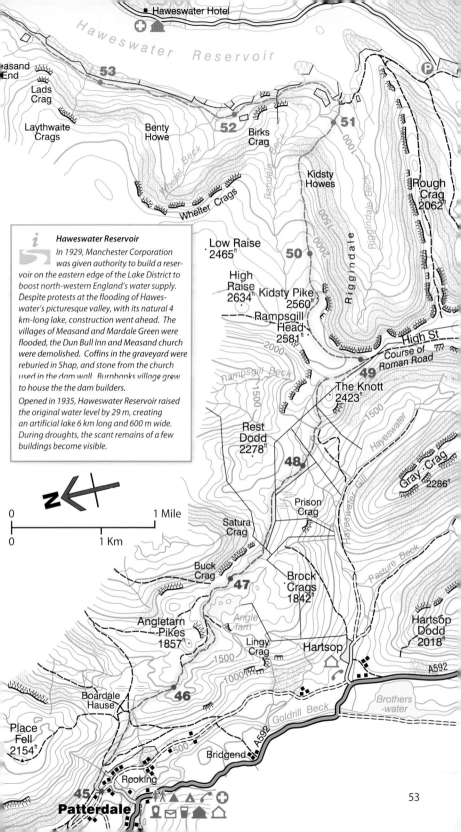

Haweswater Hotel

Haweswater Reservoir

53

asand End

Lads Crag

Laythwaite Crags

Benty Howe

52

Birks Crag

51

Whelter Crags

Kidsty Howes

Rough Crag 2062ft

Whelter Beck

Randale Beck

Riggindale Beck

Haweswater Reservoir

In 1929, Manchester Corporation was given authority to build a reservoir on the eastern edge of the Lake District to boost north-western England's water supply. Despite protests at the flooding of Haweswater's picturesque valley, with its natural 4 km-long lake, construction went ahead. The villages of Measand and Mardale Green were flooded, the Dun Bull Inn and Measand church were demolished. Coffins in the graveyard were reburied in Shap, and stone from the church used in the dam wall. Burnbanks village grew to house the the dam builders.

Opened in 1935, Haweswater Reservoir raised the original water level by 29 m, creating an artificial lake 6 km long and 600 m wide. During droughts, the scant remains of a few buildings become visible.

Low Raise 2465ft

50

High Raise 2634ft

Kidsty Pike 2560ft

Rampsgill Head 2581ft

High St

Course of Roman Road

49

The Knott 2423ft

Riggindale

Haweswater

Rampsgill Beck

Rest Dodd 2278ft

48

Gray Crag 2286ft

N

0 ——— 1 Mile
0 ——— 1 Km

Prison Crag

Satura Crag

Haweswater Gill

Pasture Beck

Buck Crag

47

Brock Crags 1842ft

Hartsop Dodd 2018ft

Angletarn Pikes 1857ft

Angle Tarn

Lingy Crag

Hartsop

A592

Brothers -water

46

Boardale Hause

Goldrill Beck

Place Fell 2154ft

Bridgend

A592

Rooking

45

Patterdale

- Beyond a gap in a stone wall, the outlook changes: a wide valley and plains beyond extend almost to the horizon. Keep a wall or fence in sight on your right. The stony path crosses a small plateau, then Hayeswater appears below.

- Descend through a gap in the wall, then climb, soon crossing boggy ground. Ford a small steam and continue uphill, through a low wall, then pass below the amorphous lump of The Knott.

- A short distance down the path, bear sharp left at a large cairn, along a clear path. A fine ridge walk takes you to the summit of Kidsty Pike. At 780m/2560ft, it's the highest point on the entire walk.

- The Pennines, to be crossed in a few days' time, are draped across the eastern horizon. In the intermediate distance, beyond Haweswater Reservoir far below, Shap quarry is unmistakeable. If it's clear, you may see Morecambe Bay to the south and the Solway Firth to the north.

- The upper reaches of the steep descent follow a path made during 2009. Its builders hope that the disturbed ground will recover within a few years. It's particularly steep through and below a band of rocks.

- Once you are down almost to the level of Haweswater Reservoir (see panel on page 53), cross a bridge over Randale Beck. The path onwards, above the reservoir, is always clear. It's punctuated by some steep undulations, notably below Whelter Crags, but there are not many boggy bits and some pleasant stretches through mature woodlands.

- From the bridge over Measand Beck, a track leads on. Beyond a point where you're level with the reservoir wall, go right at a fork and down to a gate. Descend a little further, then bear left to a minor road and on to the main road in the hamlet of Burnbanks.

- Here an information panel outlines how it has developed from a model settlement for workers constructing the reservoir in the 1930s. Cross the road directly to a signposted path through woodland, the first C2C sign for some time.

Kidsty Pike

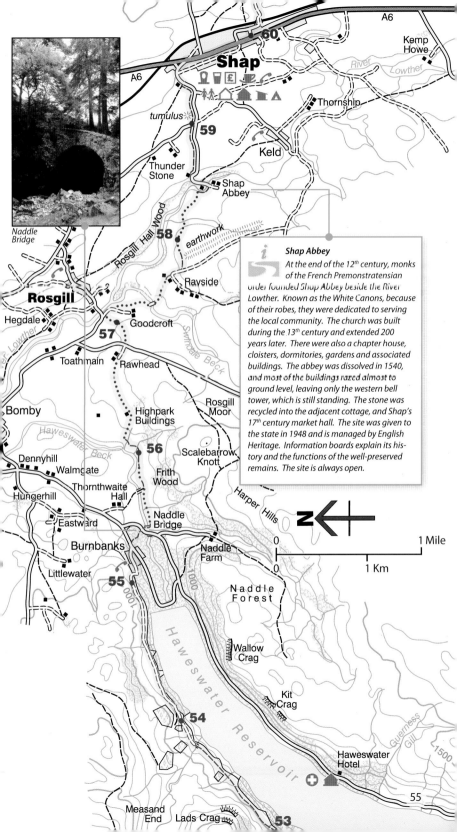

A6

Shap

60

Kemp Howe

River Lowther

A6

Thornship

tumulus

59

Keld

Thunder Stone

Shap Abbey

Naddle Bridge

Rosgill Hall Wood

58

earthwork

Rayside

Rosgill

Hegdale

Goodcroft

57

Swindale Beck

Toathmain

Rawhead

Bomby

Highpark Buildings

Rosgill Moor

Haweswater Beck

56

Scalebarrow Knott

Dennyhill

Walmgate

Frith Wood

Thornthwaite Hall

Hungerhill

Naddle Bridge

Harper Hills

Eastward

Burnbanks

Naddle Farm

Littlewater

55

1000

Naddle Forest

Z ⟵

0   1 Mile

0   1 Km

Haweswater Reservoir

Wallow Crag

Kit Crag

Guerness Gill

54

Haweswater Hotel

55

1500

Measand End

Lads Crag

53

i Shap Abbey

At the end of the 12th century, monks of the French Premonstratensian order founded Shap Abbey beside the River Lowther. Known as the White Canons, because of their robes, they were dedicated to serving the local community. The church was built during the 13th century and extended 200 years later. There were also a chapter house, cloisters, dormitories, gardens and associated buildings. The abbey was dissolved in 1540, and most of the buildings razed almost to ground level, leaving only the western bell tower, which is still standing. The stone was recycled into the adjacent cottage, and Shap's 17th century market hall. The site was given to the state in 1948 and is managed by English Heritage. Information boards explain its history and the functions of the well-preserved remains. The site is always open.

- Next, cross another road to a stile and go over the old stone-built Naddle Bridge, then a footbridge. Bear left along a clear path beside the stream.
- After half a mile (about 800 m) the path leaves the stream and rises beside a small tributary. Cross this, go over a stile and right up the field, as indicated.
- Pass Highpark, a low stone building, and cross a field dotted with mature trees. More stiles separate another two fields. Then go through a gate to a house access road and on to a minor road.
- Cross and continue towards Rosgill Bridge. Descend to a stile, and on its far side, bear right to a gate.
- Follow a signposted path between a stone wall and Swindale Beck. Shortly, go through a gate on the right. Bear left along a faint path beside the stone wall.
- A clear path now crosses a field to a small stone bridge over Swindale Beck. Walk up the field to another stile built into the wall.
- Pass derelict farm buildings and go through a gate to a minor road. Walk uphill for about 100 m, then turn left through a gate as indicated.
- Cross a field, go through a small gate, then bear diagonally right across the next field, aiming for the corner of a stone wall. As you reach a crest, Shap Abbey comes into view.
- Descend to a stile, crossing a small stream en route. Cross the next field towards a point just left of the abbey. The path leads to a stone wall on the left, just above a stream.
- Cross a stile. To visit the abbey, turn right here, then retrace your steps to head for Shap: see panel on page 55.
- Next, go through a gate and across a footbridge to a minor road. Near the top of a rise, bear left up to a stile, then walk along a field edge.
- Cross a road then go on through the next two fields to a gate on the right. This minor road leads into the village of Shap.

Shap Abbey

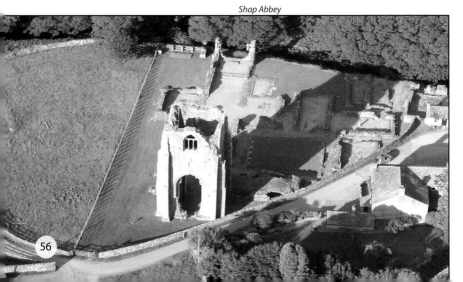

5 Shap to Orton

Distance	**8 miles (12.9 km)**
Terrain	**minor roads, field paths to quarry road, then tracks, paths, minor road, and finally field paths into Orton**
Food and drink	**none between Shap and Orton**
Summary	**undulating route through beautiful limestone pavement countryside with wide views to the attractive village of Orton**

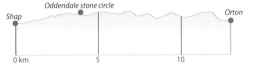

- Set out along Shap's main road. Turn left along Moss Grove then right, as indicated, at an intersection. This minor road becomes a track, bending left to a railway bridge.

- On the far side, follow the route between fields; a path joins from the left. Continue to a stile over a stone wall.

- A clear path across fields takes you to the footbridge high above the busy M6. Yesterday, from Kidsty Pike you could see Shap cement works (to the right from here) – a satisfying, if unlovely, measure of progress.

- Continue beside a fence, through hawthorn bushes. As the path starts to rise away from the motorway, traverse a field to a gate and descend to cross a minor road.

- Follow a track to Oddendale across a field and below limestone crags. It bends left, uphill, with a stone wall on the right. Walk along the top of the crags, descend to some steps, cross the quarry access road and go up to a track.

North over Orton

- It leads to a T-junction where you turn right then, in a dip, go right again as indicated along a track. Soon, at a junction, continue on a clearer track, across fields and slightly uphill.

- Beyond some trees and a field on the right, go down to the corner of a small plantation, then up across a field. The nearby Roman road shown on the map is indistinct, but at least you know that the Romans marched past here too. Follow waymarkers along a path, aiming for a post on the skyline.

- Pass through a fascinating area of classic limestone pavement (see page 20) and down. Soon you pass a very large granite boulder, transported here during the last Ice Age and left behind when the ice thawed: see page 21.

- Descend to cross a small stream then go up to the corner of a stone wall. Bear left and up, with a wall on the left. The route undulates sharply, across steep-sided clefts and up to a crest. The so-called Robin Hood's Grave lies about 150 m south of the route, but there's no apparent access.

- Drop down from the corner of a stone wall and cross a stile to a road. Follow it to a junction and turn right. With the next junction in sight, diverge right along a short signposted path. Go over a stile to the B6260 road and cross to the signposted track to Orton.

- Within 150 m, descend past a well-preserved limekiln on the left. Go through a farmyard and cross a field. Beyond a gate, continue beside a stream.

- Soon, cross a footbridge then another field, a beautiful flower-rich hay meadow in early summer. Beyond a gate, walk beside the stream briefly. Continue across a field to a path between stone walls.

- The path bends left, down to a lane, then a T-junction. Go right, into the village of Orton. Turn right at the next junction, then left to the village centre: see panel opposite.

Ruins of limekiln beside the route

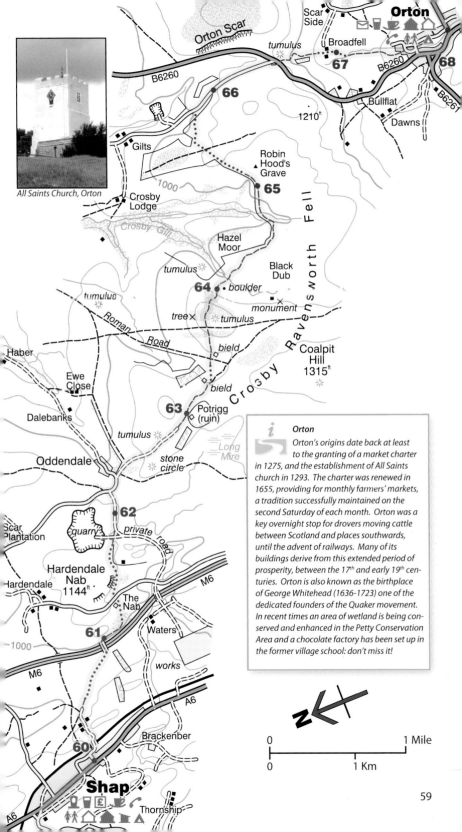

All Saints Church, Orton

Orton

Scar Side
Broadfell

Orton Scar
tumulus
67

B6260

68

B6260

B6261

66

Bullflat

1210ᶠᵗ

Dawns

Gilts

Robin Hood's Grave

1000

65

Ravensworth Fell

Crosby Lodge

Crosby Gill

Hazel Moor

Black Dub

tumulus

64 • *boulder*

monument ✕

tumulus

tree ✕ *tumulus*

Roman Road

bield

Coalpit Hill 1315ᶠᵗ

Haber

Ewe Close

bield

Dalebanks

63 Potrigg (ruin)

tumulus

Long Mire

Oddendale

stone circle

Scar Plantation

quarry

private road

62

Hardendale Nab 1144ᶠᵗ

Hardendale

The Nab

M6

61

Waters

1000

works

M6

A6

Brackenber

60

Shap

Thornship

A6

ⓘ **Orton**

Orton's origins date back at least to the granting of a market charter in 1275, and the establishment of All Saints church in 1293. The charter was renewed in 1655, providing for monthly farmers' markets, a tradition successfully maintained on the second Saturday of each month. Orton was a key overnight stop for drovers moving cattle between Scotland and places southwards, until the advent of railways. Many of its buildings derive from this extended period of prosperity, between the 17th and early 19th centuries. Orton is also known as the birthplace of George Whitehead (1636-1723) one of the dedicated founders of the Quaker movement. In recent times an area of wetland is being conserved and enhanced in the Petty Conservation Area and a chocolate factory has been set up in the former village school: don't miss it!

---

0   1 Mile
0   1 Km

6 Orton to Kirkby Stephen

Distance	**13.5 miles (21.7 km)**
Terrain	**quiet road, field paths, minor road, farm tracks, moorland track, field paths and minor roads to Kirkby Stephen**
Food and drink	**none between Orton and Kirkby Stephen**
Summary	**a moorland day of wide open spaces, punctuated by secluded Smardale; route finally descends through farmland to a busy market town**

- Set out along the main road in Orton, passing Petty Hall Conservation Area, opposite the fine 17th century building of the same name. Turn left along the road signposted to Raisbeck. Follow this quiet road for ¾ mile (1.2 km), then turn left across a field, as signposted, towards Knott Lane.

- Over a stile and a few steps left, turn right towards Acres. Aim for a stone barn near tall trees, keeping close to the stone wall on the right. After three gates and a stile, pass the barn.

- Continue through fields separated by four gates to a minor road opposite Acres Farm and turn left. Go past Sunbiggin Farm on the left. At the next farm, follow a track straight on towards Sunbiggin Tarn.

- Here you will see the first of several informative signs about the recommended route through Open Access Land: see page 111 for contact details.

- The track drops slightly to a junction, and turn right. Descend to a minor road, for another right turn.

- Follow this for 500 m, then turn left. Be sure to turn left again 250 m further on, avoiding the temptingly clear way straight on. Sunbiggin Tarn should be visible half a mile to the north.

- Go through a gate to follow a fairly well-defined grassy track, leading generally south-east. It could be muddy, although a short footbridge crosses the worst of it.

Between Orton and Sunbiggin Tarn

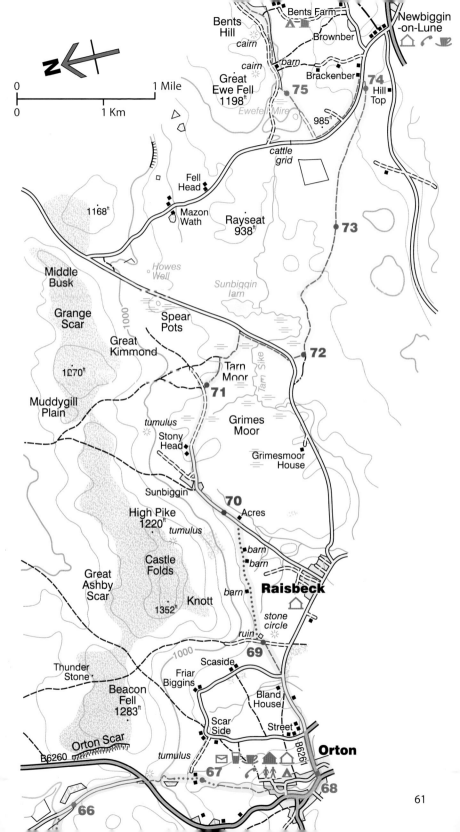

Bents Farm
Newbiggin-on-Lune
Bents Hill
Brownber
cairn
barn
Brackenber
cairn
Great Ewe Fell
1198ft
75
74
Hill Top
Ewefell Mire
985ft
cattle grid
73
Fell Head
1168ft
Mazon Wath
Rayseat
938ft
Howes Well
Middle Busk
Sunbiggin Tarn
Grange Scar
Spear Pots
Great Kimmond
72
1070ft
Tarn Moor
71
Tarn Sike
Muddygill Plain
tumulus
Grimes Moor
Stony Head
Grimesmoor House
Sunbiggin
70
Acres
High Pike
1220ft
tumulus
barn
barn
Castle Folds
Raisbeck
Great Ashby Scar
barn
Knott
1352ft
stone circle
ruin
69
Thunder Stone
Scaside
Beacon Fell
1283ft
Friar Biggins
Bland House
Scar Side
Street
B6261
Orton
Orton Scar
B6260
tumulus
67
68
66

0 — 1 Mile
0 — 1 Km

61

- The track gains height to a crest from where a field enclosed by a stone wall is a crucial guide: keep it close on your left and continue down slightly to a minor road.

- Turn left then right along a track, soon passing a reservoir. Ignore a path to the right, and continue along the pleasant grassy track, above Bents Farm.

- As the track becomes fainter, follow the stone wall on the right downhill. Beyond a gate and stile, walkers are asked to stay close to the wall to protect Severals, an Iron Age settlement nearby: see page 26. Its scant remains – stony outlines of enclosures and small huts – are best seen from the ensuing steep descent.

- Turn right at a deserted stone building, then left through a gate and over the track of a one-time railway to follow a path to the right. Descend, bear left to cross Scandal Beck by Smardale Bridge and turn up a track signposted to Kirkby Stephen.

- Soon there's a good view of Smardale Gill old viaduct to the north: see page 28. Keep climbing, go through a gate and turn left, keeping a stone wall on your left.

- Gaining a crest, bear left (with the stone wall on your left) and descend on a walker-friendly grassy track. If visibility is good, you may be able to spot a row of tiny dots on the eastern skyline. They're the cairns of Nine Standards, which you'll reach tomorrow.

- Go through a gate to a road and turn right, then shortly left. About 150 m along, go over a stone wall on the right, as indicated.

- Cross a field and go through a railway underpass. Traversing the next field, aim for some trees and a marker post.

- Then it's downhill following the waymarkers, through a gap in the fence and across a small valley. The clear path leads to a stone wall and line of trees. Cross a stile and descend another field.

- Go through another underpass and turn left to avoid the farmyard, keeping to a well-marked route that soon curves right, to a minor road. Turn left to reach some houses.

- Follow a lane behind them, and turn right opposite a play area to reach the main road in Kirkby Stephen: see panel opposite.

Smardale Bridge

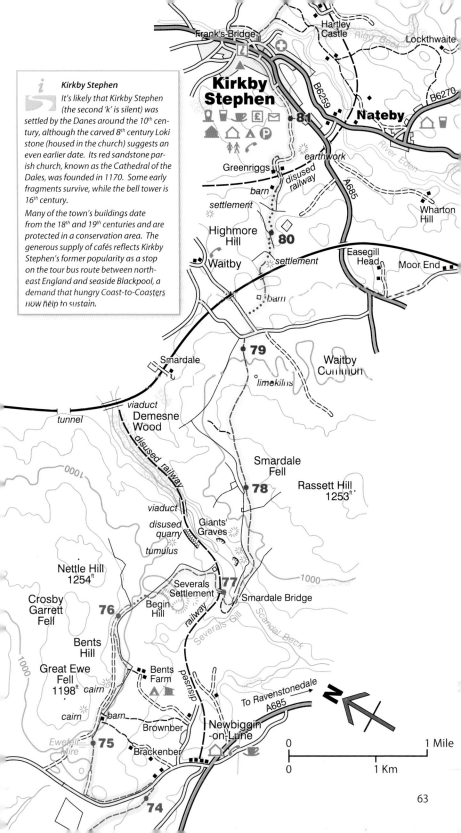

Kirkby Stephen

It's likely that Kirkby Stephen (the second 'k' is silent) was settled by the Danes around the 10th century, although the carved 8th century Loki stone (housed in the church) suggests an even earlier date. Its red sandstone parish church, known as the Cathedral of the Dales, was founded in 1170. Some early fragments survive, while the bell tower is 16th century.

Many of the town's buildings date from the 18th and 19th centuries and are protected in a conservation area. The generous supply of cafés reflects Kirkby Stephen's former popularity as a stop on the tour bus route between north-east England and seaside Blackpool, a demand that hungry Coast-to-Coasters now help to sustain.

Frank's Bridge

Hartley Castle

Lockthwaite

Rigg Beck

Kirkby Stephen

B6259

B6270

Nateby

81

River Eden

earthwork

Greenriggs

disused railway

barn

A685

settlement

Wharton Hill

Highmore Hill

80

settlement

Easegill Head

Moor End

Waitby

barn

79

Smardale

Waitby Common

°limekilns

tunnel

viaduct

Demesne Wood

disused railway

Smardale Fell

Rassett Hill 1253ft

78

viaduct

disused quarry

Giants' Graves

tumulus

Nettle Hill 1254ft

1000

Severals Settlement

77

Crosby Garrett Fell

76

Begin Hill

Smardale Bridge

railway

Severals Gill

Scandal Beck

Bents Hill

Great Ewe Fell 1198ft cairn

Bents Farm

disused

N

cairn

barn

To Ravenstonedale
A685

Ewefell Mire

75

Brownber

Newbiggin -on-Lune

Brackenber

0 ——— 1 Mile

0 ——— 1 Km

74

7 Kirkby Stephen to Keld

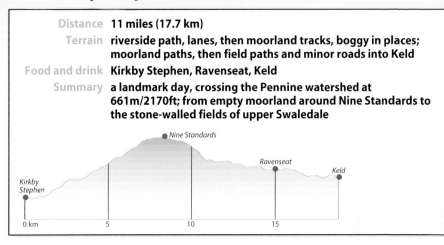

Distance	**11 miles (17.7 km)**
Terrain	**riverside path, lanes, then moorland tracks, boggy in places; moorland paths, then field paths and minor roads into Keld**
Food and drink	**Kirkby Stephen, Ravenseat, Keld**
Summary	**a landmark day, crossing the Pennine watershed at 661m/2170ft; from empty moorland around Nine Standards to the stone-walled fields of upper Swaledale**

- Follow the main road through Kirkby Stephen. Bear right on the far side of the tourist information office to cross Market Square. Turn right along a lane, following a sign to Frank's Bridge, down Stoneshot.

- Go left down steps and left to cross the 16th century bridge, on the ancient corpse route along which coffins were carried from neighbouring villages. Continue along a riverside path, then a surfaced path up across a field. Bear slightly left to a path into Hartley.

- Turn right for about 50 m, then left down a path and across a footbridge. Turn right along the road, which climbs steeply, becoming a track past Hartley quarries.

- The track maintains the ascent, with views westwards of the Lake District mountains as due reward. Eventually you reach a junction with a sign indicating the direct route to Nine Standards to the left.

- The faint track to the right is the 'green' winter route, to be used December to April or in bad weather at any time of year. Seasonal routes have been established to minimise erosion of the fragile moorland.

The Nine Standards

87 ●

Rowber Edge

Millstones

B6270

White Mossy Hill

Coldbergh Edge

Coldbergh Side

2000

Route from August to November

Black Hill

Birk Dale

86 ●
trig. point

Nine Standards Rigg 2170ft

Nine Standards ▲

view indicator

Route from May to July

Bastifell 2024ft

2000

Faraday Gill

Route from May to November

85 ●

1500

Dukerdale

Rigg Beck

Route from December to April

Tailbridge Hill 1796ft

B6270

Hartley Fell

Greenfell Crag

Nateby Common

▲ *barn ruin*

84 ●

1324ft

Ladthwaite

Long Rigg
1356ft

Birkett Beck

Fell House ●

83 ●
1000

quarry

Low Out Wood

Lockthwaite

Rigg Beck

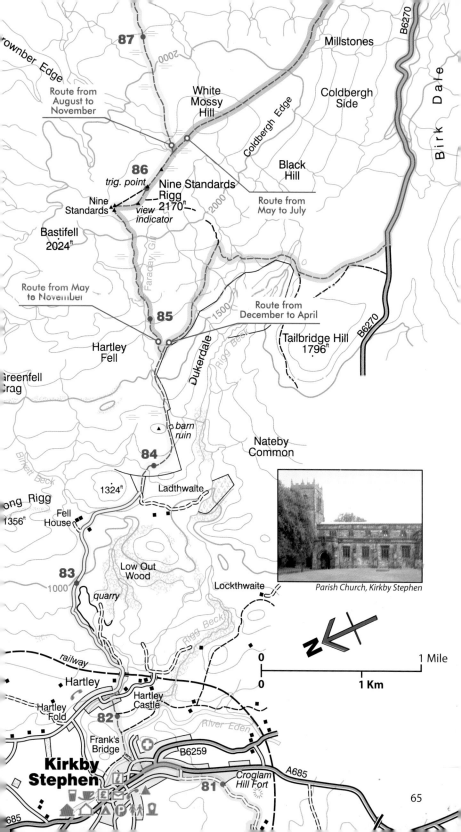

Parish Church, Kirkby Stephen

N

0 ———————————————— 1 Mile
0 ———————————————— 1 Km

railway

Hartley

Hartley Castle

82 ●

Hartley Fold

Frank's Bridge

✚

Kirkby Stephen

B6259

River Eden

A685

Croglam Hill Fort

81 ●

685

May to November (red and blue routes)

- The path climbs to the amazing group of cairns, Nine Standards, an ideal place for a break. These superb examples of the cairn builder's art, most dating from the 18th century or earlier, probably originated as county boundary markers. A view indicator a little further east identifies about 50 hills and mountains by name, direction and altitude.

- Continue, turning south, past a triangulation pillar, through peaty ground, to a junction. Bear right for the 'red' route during May to July, or left on the 'blue' route between August and November. *Blue route continues on page 68, red route on page 69*

December to April (green route)

- Refer to the map on page 65: the green route turns off right shortly before mile 85 at a junction that may have a seasonal marker. It's just above two prominent stone cairns on your left. The faint trodden path heads south at first, soon confirmed by a low timber post but (in 2009) no waymarker.

- The path veers south-east, uphill across the moorland. After over half a mile (1 km) take a sharp right turn (waymarked) and descend past the cairn shown below. The route curves downhill, parallel to the stone wall, and dips to cross Rigg Beck.

- After rising briefly, the grassy path continues its gentle descent to the road, passing a large tarn on the left before crossing some limestone pavement. The path becomes a track, veering left (south) to meet the B6270.

- Turn left to follow the road, soon descending eastwards into Birkdale. After 2.5 miles (4 km), you'll see a fingerpost on the left with a map of seasonal routes. However, it points up a steep, awkward landslip, and it's much easier to continue 100 m and turn left up the vehicle track.

- After the track gives out, maintain an easterly heading along the fairly well-defined path (no waymarkers in 2009). Within 700 m, the green and red routes merge at a junction that may be signposted.

Cairn below the right turn

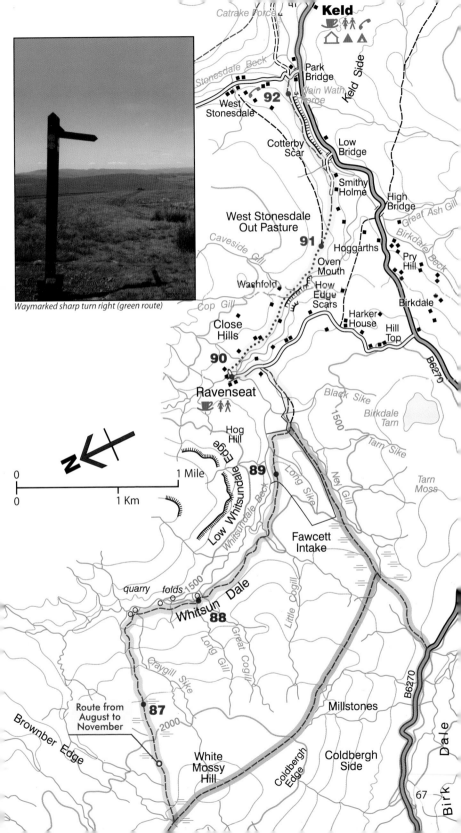

Waymarked sharp turn right (green route)

Catrake Force
Keld
Keld Side

Stonesdale Beck

Park Bridge
92
West Stonesdale
Wain Wath Force

Cotterby Scar
Low Bridge

Smithy Holme

High Bridge
Great Ash Gill

West Stonesdale Out Pasture
91
Hoggarths
Birkdale Beck
Pry Hill

Caveside Gill
Oven Mouth

Washfold
How Edge Scars
Birkdale

Cop Gill
Close Hills
Harker House
Hill Top

90
Ravenseat
B6270

Black Sike
Birkdale Tarn

Hog Hill
1500
Tarn Sike
Tarn Moss

N

Low Whitsundale Edge
Whitsundale Beck
89
Long Sike
Ney Gill

Fawcett Intake

0   1 Mile
0   1 Km

quarry   folds 1500
Whitsun Dale
88
Little Cogill

Long Gill
Great Cogill

Graygill Sike

Route from August to November
87
2000
Millstones
B6270

Brownber Edge

White Mossy Hill
Coldbergh Edge
Coldbergh Side

Birk Dale

67

Blue route (August to November)

Waymarker for the blue route

- About 500 m beyond Nine Standards trig point, where the route passes through peat hags, turn left (east) for the blue route. The timber waymarker poles are intermittent and in places discreet to the point of invisible. The going is boggy in places and the descent barely noticeable at first.

- After over a mile (2 km) the descent becomes steeper, views open up to the south-east and the route swings right (south) to follow the valley of Whitsundale Beck. Follow the beck downstream, mainly alongside it but latterly at a higher level through a section where heather is regenerating.

- After about 2 miles (3 km) of valley, you reach a right turn marked by fingerpost. Within 150 m, turn left at the confluence of the three routes, just above Ravenseat Farm.

Whitsundale Beck (blue route)

Red route (May to July)

- The path leads on across the grass and peat hags, over White Mossy Hill and almost featureless moor. From a large pile of stones, the descent begins in earnest and the valley below begins to open up. You pass Millstones cairn, then a tiny footbridge.

- The path continues down to a well-drained track, where the winter route joins after its climb from the B6270. However, the track soon ends at a locked shed.

- It resumes, after a fashion, about 100 m further on. Pass a row of neatly built shooting butts (shelters), used during the grouse season from mid-August.

- The path continues down, soon with a fence on the left, to a vehicle track and the junction with the autumn route. Go down to a road and turn left to Ravenseat Farm.

- Cross a footbridge on the right and go through a gate, across a field to another gate and straight on beside a stream. Beyond the next gate, turn uphill towards a stone barn.

- Pass this barn, and the next, and follow the path past the next barn to the left. Yellow waymarkers indicate the direction through a gateway and onwards through more gates and fields, above a gorge on the River Swale below.

- Further on, the route crosses open, sometimes boggy ground. Drop down to a house, soon on a better path which swings left in front of the house and goes down, through a gate.

- Pass a derelict house, descend through a gateway and bear left along a path, shaded by trees, with a stone wall on the right. Cross various stiles and a footbridge to reach a gate and turn right down to a road.

- Continue to the main road and turn left. Soon, turn left down a minor road, signposted Keld Only, and go downhill. Turn left at a T-junction in Keld village centre: see panel.

> ### *i* Keld
>
> Keld can trace its origins to Norse times, its name meaning spring or stream. Little is known of its history. A corpse or coffin road crossed the slopes of Kisdon Hill, overlooking it to the south-east, leading to Grinton near Reeth. This road was re-routed in 1580 along what is now the Pennine Way, just bypassing Keld to reach a new church at Muker, downstream beside the River Swale.
>
> Many of Keld's existing buildings date from the mid-19th century lead mining era, including the two former Methodist chapels. Its peaceful atmosphere these days perhaps belies its importance as both the halfway mark on the Coast to Coast, and as a staging point on the Pennine Way.

Ravenseat Farm

8 Keld to Reeth

Distance	**10½ miles (16.9 km)**
Terrain	**tracks and paths – rough, wet and steep in places; field paths and tracks above Swaledale; rough path, then short road into Reeth**
Food and drink	**none between Keld and Reeth**
Summary	**switchback route through the stark, fascinating remains of lead mining, in sharp contrast to farmland and woodlands of Swaledale below; low-level alternative available**

Keld — Blakethwaite — Surrender Bridge — Reeth

0 km   5   10   15

- Set out northwards through Keld. At a T-junction, turn right along the path to Muker. Soon, bear left down the Pennine Way, as indicated, to cross a bridge with a good view of East Gill Force.

- Bear left and up to a junction then right across another, larger bridge and up briefly. Further on, with marvellous views of Swaledale, pass an old barn on the right.

- To keep to the high-level Wainwright route, bear left within 100 m along a path beside a relic of mining days. The low-level alternative route is described on page 75.

East Gill Force

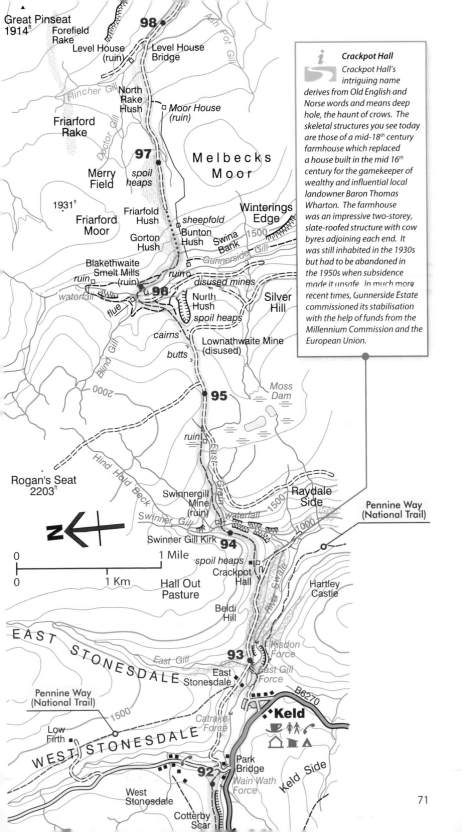

Great Pinseat
1914ft
Forefield
Rake
Level House
(ruin)
Level House
Bridge

98

Ash Pot Gill

Flincher Gill

North
Rake
Hush

Moor House
(ruin)

Friarford
Rake

Doctor Gill

M e l b e c k s
M o o r

97

Merry
Field

spoil
heaps

1931ft

Friarford
Moor

Friarfold
Hush

sheepfold

Gorton
Hush

Bunton
Hush

Winterings
Edge

Swina
Bank

1500

Gunnerside Gill

Blakethwaite
Smelt Mills
(ruin)

ruin

ruin

disused mines

98

waterfall

flue

North
Hush

Silver
Hill

spoil heaps

Blind Gill

cairns

butts

Lownathwaite Mine
(disused)

2000

95

Moss
Dam

Rogan's Seat
2203ft

ruin

East Grain

Hind Hold Beck

Swinnergill
Mine
(ruin)

Raydale
Side

1500

1000

Swinner Gill

waterfall

Pennine Way
(National Trail)

Swinner Gill Kirk

94

spoil heaps

Hall Out
Pasture

Crackpot
Hall

River Swale

Hartley
Castle

Beldi
Hill

ℹ *Crackpot Hall*

Crackpot Hall's intriguing name derives from Old English and Norse words and means deep hole, the haunt of crows. The skeletal structures you see today are those of a mid-18th century farmhouse which replaced a house built in the mid 16th century for the gamekeeper of wealthy and influential local landowner Baron Thomas Wharton. The farmhouse was an impressive two-storey, slate-roofed structure with cow byres adjoining each end. It was still inhabited in the 1930s but had to be abandoned in the 1950s when subsidence made it unsafe. In much more recent times, Gunnerside Estate commissioned its stabilisation with the help of funds from the Millennium Commission and the European Union.

EAST
STONESDALE

East Gill

93

Kisdon
Force

East
Stonesdale

East Gill
Force

B6270

Pennine Way
(National Trail)

1500

Catrake
Force

Keld

Low
Firth

WEST STONESDALE

92

Park
Bridge

Keld Side

West
Stonesdale

Wain Wath
Force

Cotterby
Scar

Z ⭠

0 ——————————— 1 Mile
0 ——————————— 1 Km

- Gain height, bending left above the ruins of Crackpot Hall, dating from the 17th century and abandoned only in the 1950s: see panel. Pass a more substantial stone building as you follow a clear track, through a gate.

Stone wall of Blakethwaite peat store

- Within 50 m, cross broken rock slabs and continue on a path, down and across Swinner Gill to pass between two ruinous buildings.

- The narrow path leads up East Grain, close to the stream, and is generally steep and rocky, in places boggy or heathery. Up on the moors, bear right and go on up to a junction with a track to Rogan's Seat.

- Descend to a junction marked with two cairns and turn left along a path. It descends steeply, across two streams to Blakethwaite and the well-preserved skeleton of the peat store.

- Keeping the peat store on your right, climb to a track and turn right, then sharp left at the next junction. Continue across mining spoil to open moorland.

- Go on up to a vehicle track and turn right. Next comes an extensive area of rather bleak, bare spoil, but once you start to descend, patches of heather brighten the scene.

Blakethwaite mining area

Mile

72

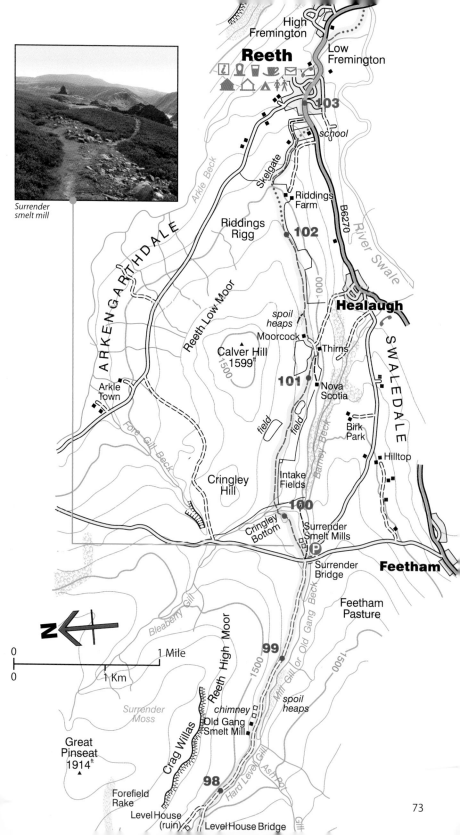

Surrender smelt mill

High Fremington

Reeth

Low Fremington

103

school

Skelgate

Riddings Farm

Riddings Rigg

102

Arkle Beck

B6270

River Swale

ARKENGARTHDALE

Reeth Low Moor

spoil heaps

Moorcock

Healaugh

Thirns

Calver Hill
1599ft

101

Nova Scotia

SWALEDALE

1500

Fore Gill Beck

Arkle Town

field

field

Birk Park

Barney Beck

Hilltop

Cringley Hill

Intake Fields

100

Cringley Bottom

Surrender Smelt Mills

P

Surrender Bridge

Feetham

Feetham Pasture

Bleaberry Gill

Reeth High Moor

Mill Gill or Old Gang Beck

N

1500

1500

0   1 Mile

0   1 Km

99

spoil heaps

Surrender Moss

chimney

Old Gang Smelt Mill

Great Pinseat
1914ft

Crag Willas

98

Hard Level Gill

Askrigg

Gill

Forefield Rake

Level House (ruin)

Level House Bridge

73

- Descend steadily, cross Level House Bridge and go on beside Hard Level Gill to reach the Old Gang mining site with its landmark tall chimney. Continue across a road near Surrender Bridge, and follow a track above Surrender smelt mills.

- Maintain height on the path across boggy ground. Cairns mark the way across moorland and down to Cringley Bottom. Climb to a moorland path, at first with a stone wall on your right.

- Soon the track starts to descend. Past Thirns Farm, bear left and up past Moorcock to the moors. Eventually you start to lose height. At a left bend, continue straight on along a grassy path above Riddings Farm.

- Go through a gate to a path between stone walls. Cross a farm track, go through a gate and turn right over a narrow stile beside another gate. Traverse a field, go through a gap in a wall to another field, then over a stile.

- Cross a small grassed area behind a school, and follow a path down to a road. Turn left along the roadside path to reach the small town of Reeth, at the confluence of Arkle Beck and the River Swale.

Old Gang smelt mill

i **Reeth**

Reeth dates back more than 1000 years. Long the market town for the local farming community, it has a beautiful central green, surrounded by fine 18th century stone buildings. It grew rapidly during the 19th century with the development of mining in the area.

For more about Reeth and its environs, visit the Swaledale museum, on the eastern side of the green. Housed in an early 19th century Methodist day school, its displays feature geology, Iron Age settlements, lead mining (17th to mid 20th centuries), music and Methodism, and vernacular building. The museum and café are open between Easter and October daily 10.30-17.30 but closed on Saturdays: **www.swaledale.org**.

War memorial beside Reeth green

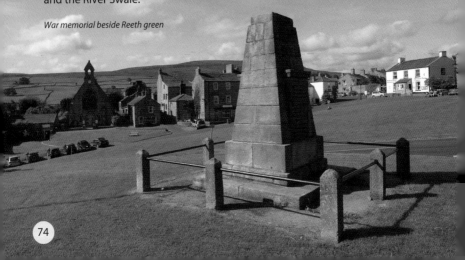

Suspension bridge over River Swale

Low-level alternative

- This riverside route through Swaledale is generally clearly defined by a string of signposted paths and some quiet roads. It offers a very attractive alternative to the high-level Wainwright route, especially in bad weather.

- At the junction marked by the mining relic shown below, continue straight on and, soon descending, drop to river level. The wide track leads on unmistakeably.

- To reach Muker, bear right with a footbridge in sight, downstream. Otherwise, continue straight on for Reeth, via Gunnerside, Ivelet and just under a mile (1.5 km) of the B6270 road.

- Once houses are in sight, the path into Reeth is signposted. Closer in, follow the route indicated by yellow waymarkers.

Mining relic marking the junction

9 Reeth to Richmond

Distance	**10½ miles (16.9 km)**
Terrain	**roadside path, river bank, minor road, forest and field paths, some quiet road, then field paths and vehicle track lead to minor road into Richmond**
Food and drink	**Reeth, Nun Cote Nook, Richmond**
Summary	**a varied route down Swaledale, with a steep ascent to Marrick and undulations through fields and woods below the impressive cliffs of Applegarth Scar, down to historic town of Richmond**

- Follow the main road out of Reeth, down and across a bridge. A little further on, diverge to a path to Grinton beside a tributary of the River Swale. It leads across a field and up to a road.

- Cross the road, turning slightly left then right down to a track. This pleasant path follows the river for half a mile (under 1 km) to a stile where you turn right along a minor road.

- After about 50 m you pass the entrance to Marrick Priory, now an outdoor education centre: see panel opposite. Go left through a gate and up a wide grassy path into woodland, signposted to Marrick.

- The path climbs steadily to a gate. Continue on a field path with a stone wall on the right. Go through three gates to a minor road. Follow it around a left bend and turn right at the next two junctions.

- Almost at the end of the tarmac, with Park Lodge on your left, turn left along a path to Hollins Farm. A succession of field paths, separated by gates, takes you up to a crest then down to the track to Nun Cote Nook.

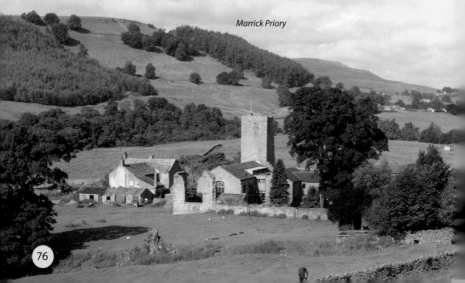

Marrick Priory

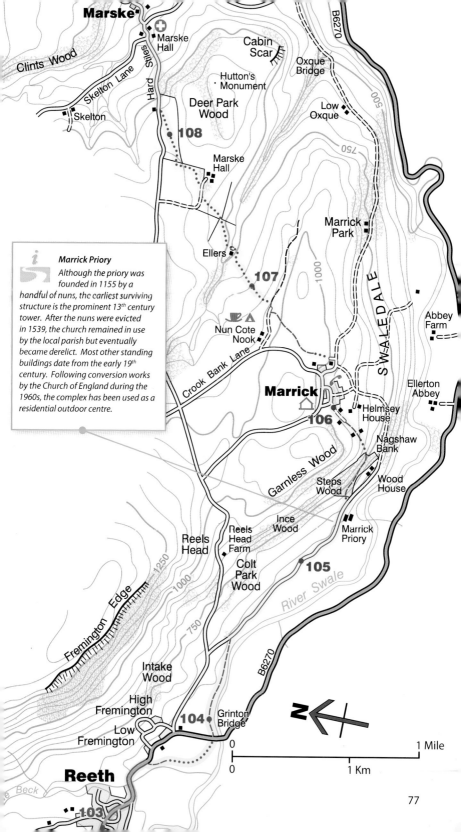

Marske

Clints Wood

Marske Hall

Skelton Lane

Hard Stiles

Cabin Scar

B6270

Oxque Bridge

Hutton's Monument

Skelton

Deer Park Wood

108

Low Oxque

500

Marske Hall

750

Marrick Park

Ellers

107

1000

SWALEDALE

Abbey Farm

Marrick Priory

Although the priory was founded in 1155 by a handful of nuns, the earliest surviving structure is the prominent 13th century tower. After the nuns were evicted in 1539, the church remained in use by the local parish but eventually became derelict. Most other standing buildings date from the early 19th century. Following conversion works by the Church of England during the 1960s, the complex has been used as a residential outdoor centre.

Nun Cote Nook

Crook Bank Lane

Marrick

106

Helmsey House

Ellerton Abbey

Nagshaw Bank

Garnless Wood

Steps Wood

Wood House

Ince Wood

Reels Head

Reels Head Farm

Colt Park Wood

Marrick Priory

105

River Swale

1250

Fremington Edge

1000

Intake Wood

750

High Fremington

104

Grinton Bridge

B6270

Low Fremington

N

Reeth

0   1 Mile

0   1 Km

e Beck

103

- Bear right then left, and follow waymarkers carefully down across fields separated by gates or stiles. Descend to a sharp left turn at Ellers Farmhouse.

- Go through a gate, across a small footbridge, then up to a power pole. Bear right across a field, through a gate, across another field, aiming for the trees ahead. Beyond a gate, turn right along a track.

- Then bear left, following yellow waymarkers, up and across a field towards a stone wall. Go over a stile where the fence and wall intersect. Go right, through a gate.

- Gain a bit of height, then descend across a field towards farm buildings. Pass through a small gate and veer right down to a road. Follow it steeply down, then turn left at a junction.

- Climb through the attractive village of Marske with its well-tended gardens. Turn right at the next junction. The next turn is right, over a stile.

- Cross fields and go through a gap in a hedge. Then it's more stiles and fields, leading to the descent to Clapgate Beck, which you cross.

St Edmund's, Marske

- A narrow path climbs steeply towards a prominent cairn of white-painted stones and meets a vehicle track. Turn right, below Applegarth Scar.

- Continue past Applegarth Low Wood, then Applegarth Farm. From a barn go straight ahead towards a stone wall, through a stile, and across two fields.

- A short distance further on, cross a minor road (to Low Applegarth) and go over a stile to the next field. Beyond two more fields and a stile, cross a minor road to East Applegarth Farm.

- Then comes another stile, field and gate, and you reach a good track. Go through a gate into Whitcliffe Wood. On its far side, join a minor road at High Leases.

- This takes you all the way down to the A6108, the main road through Richmond.

Applegarth Scar

Richmond

Richmond Bridge

Holly Hill

113

West Field

Hurgill

cemetery

112
High Leases

1047 ft

S W A L E D A L E

A6108

Whitcliffe Wood

Hudswell

1000

Scar

750

River Swale

Willance's Leap (monument)

500

fort

111

Whitcliffe

East Applegarth

Redbrow Wood

Hag Wood

Low Applegarth

barn

Salmon Gill

Starcote Wood

Deep Dale

West Applegarth

Applegarth Low Wood

Thorpe Under Stone

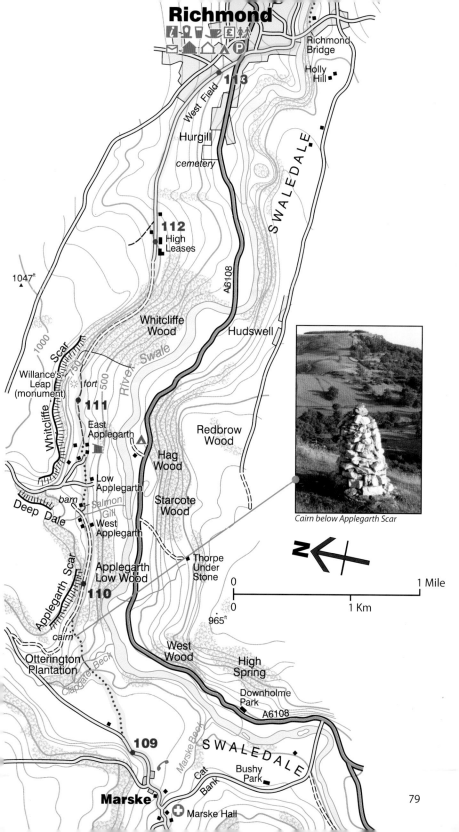

Cairn below Applegarth Scar

N

110

Applegarth Scar

cairn

Otterington Plantation

Clapgate Beck

965 ft

West Wood

High Spring

Downholme Park

A6108

0 ——— 1 Mile
0 ——— 1 Km

109

Marske Beck

S W A L E D A L E

Cat Bank

Bushy Park

Marske

Marske Hall

79

Richmond

A great place for a rest day on the C2C, Richmond's name derives from the *riche monte* (strong hill) on which it stands. Following his victory of 1066, William the Conqueror granted a huge part of Yorkshire to his kinsman Alan Rufus of Brittany. He started building Richmond's famous castle in 1071.

The keep, Richmond Castle

Its position above the River Swale is strategic, and the12th century keep dominates the town skyline. Richmond's cobbled Market Place was built within the castle's outer bounds. During the First World War, the castle was used to imprison conscientious objectors. At first, the Richmond Sixteen were sentenced to death for their pacifist stance, commuted to 10 years' hard labour. They wrote moving graffiti on their cell walls, which have been carefully preserved. The castle is open daily year-round from 10.00 to 18.00 (16.00 in winter); small admission charge, tel 01748 822 493.

In medieval times, Richmond prospered as a market town trading goods from the dales and holding fairs. It was extensively rebuilt in Georgian times, with more spacious houses and fine stone public buildings, many of which are still standing. The Town Hall (1756) is still the civic and social focus of the town. In the 1850s the covered Market Hall was built, and it still does a thriving trade today. There's plenty more at **www.richmond.org**.

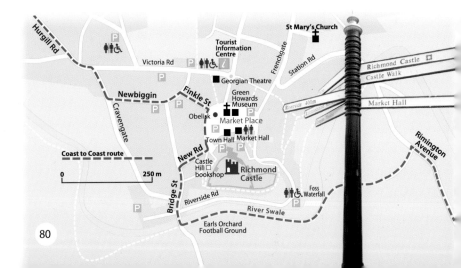

The River Swale has always been important to Richmond, and in early times its force was harnessed to power a mill to grind corn. Visit the Foss for a close view of its impressive falls. When the railway arrived in 1846, the station was located east of the Swale, partly for engineering reasons. Passenger traffic ceased in 1968, but its stonework and ironwork have been lovingly restored and repurposed: see **www.richmondstation.com**.

The excellent *Richmond Town Trail* booklet guides visitors around the town on foot. It features the highlights above, and also the Green Howards Regimental Museum (housed in old Trinity Church) and the beautifully restored Georgian Theatre Royal (1788). The booklet costs £1 (refundable against castle admission fee) from the Tourist Information Centre. The TIC is in Friary Gardens and is open daily in summer from 09.30-17.30; in winter, Monday-Saturday 09.30-16.30, tel 01748 828 742.

The suggested route for those walking through Richmond is shown in the plan opposite.

Old Trinity Church, Market Square

Market Place seen from Richmond Castle

10 Richmond to Danby Wiske

Distance	**14 miles (22.5 km)**
Terrain	**quiet roads and lanes, riverside paths and field paths, punctuated by several short sections of minor road**
Food and drink	**Richmond, Colburn, Catterick Bridge, Brompton-on-Swale, Danby Wiske**
Summary	**from River Swale to varied farmland, through two quiet villages to tranquil Danby Wiske, the route's lowest inland point at 36 m/118 ft**

- Cross Richmond Bridge, then bear left down a signposted path, soon following the Richmond Woodland Walk. Where the path divides swing right through a gate, up between two farm buildings and on to a lane.

- Past Priory Villas, turn left at a T-junction and go down to the A6136 road, cross and turn right. Follow it for 800 m to a signposted left turn.

- Follow this minor road to the entrance to the water treatment works, then bear right beside the fence. Continue straight on from the far end, across a field and into woodland.

Richmond Castle, from the River Swale

Bolton-
on-Swale

Scorton 120 Flat
Lane

Tancred
Grange

quarry

Catterick

Bainesse

gravel
quarry

River Swale

B6271

A6136

119

race
course

A1(T)

Catterick
Bridge

250

disused railway

Brough Beck

Thornbrough
Farm

Brough
Hall

118

**Brompton-
on-Swale**

House Park
Wood

Walkerville

A6136

St Giles
Farm

South Beck

117

B6271

The
Batts

Christie
Wood

Colburn

Colburn
Hall

Colburn Beck

116

Hipswell

disused
railway

250

River Swale

Red House
Farm

Hagg Farm
(ruin)

Park
Wood

B6271

Easby

abbey

Iron
Banks

115

sewage
works

**Catterick
Garrison**

A6136

Sand Beck

West
Wood

Priory
Villas

Holly
House

114

Richmond

Richmond
Bridge

Badger

113

83

N

0   1 Mile
0   1 Km

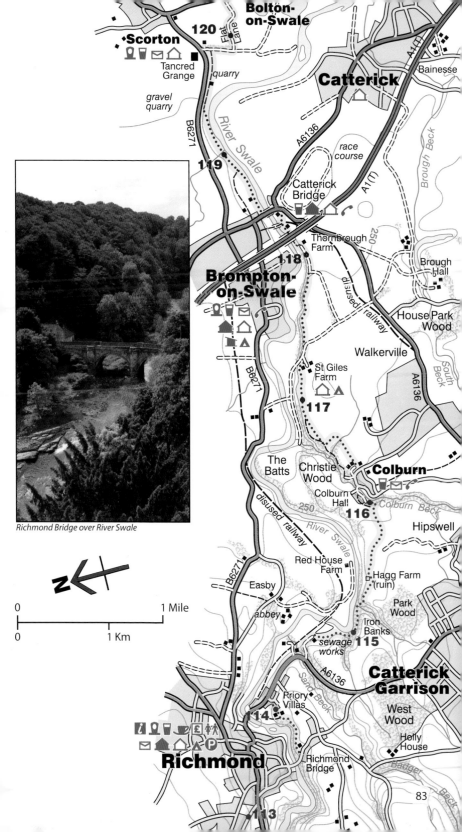

Richmond Bridge over River Swale

- Beside the river, there are some boggy bits and a narrow footbridge. As you emerge from the trees, bear left, soon passing the remains of Haggs Farm, almost buried in vegetation.

- Shortly, join a vehicle track and continue to the left. Go through a gateway, up a field to a pole. Turn left after two stiles.

- Cross a field, then go through a gate and swing left around the edge of the next field. Veer slightly left down into woodland, with a stream on the right.

- Continue to a junction, go straight on across a bridge and into the small village of Colburn.

- Pass the pub, turn right at a T-junction to a left turn, along the entrance drive to The Barn. Continue straight on, along a track with a hedge on the right.

- Turn left at the second hedge on the left, along a rough track beside a field. With a hedge on your right, veer right to a gate.

- Cross a field to an access road. Follow it for a short distance, then go through a gate and along a field edge.

- Look out for a gate on the left, leading to a succession of paths and tracks with an intervening gate, past Thornbrough Farm.

- At the end of a hard surfaced track, descend steeply left to the A1 underpass. On the far side, follow a riverbank path punctuated by stiles, under an old railway.

Bolton Beck

Danby Wiske

Danby Hill

North Farm

unter's Hill Farm

197ᶠᵗ

West Farm

Brockholme Farm

Streetlam Farm

Mossa Grange

High Brockholme

126

Fellgill Moor

Streetlam

125

B6271

Langton Grange

Moor House

White House Farm

Red House

124

The Stell

Spencer Close

Danby Plantation

Rawcar

Hewitson Hill Farm

Greenberry Farm

Stanhow

123

Ladybank House

Plumtree Moor Plantation

B6271

Kiplin

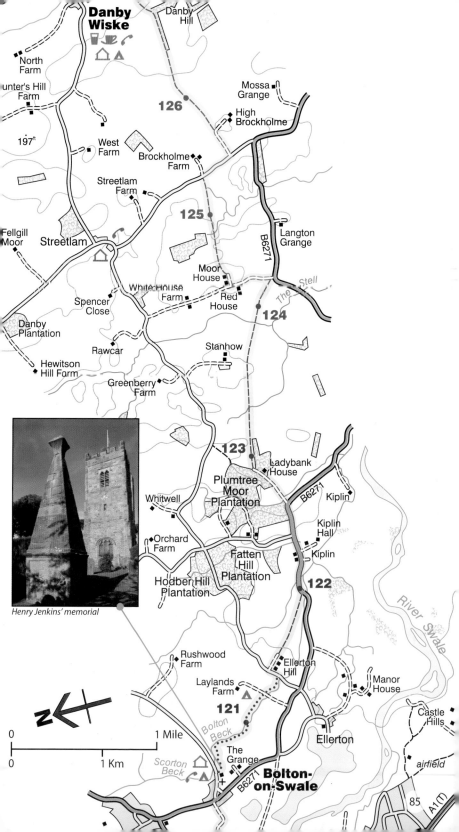

Henry Jenkins' memorial

Whitwell

Orchard Farm

Fatten Hill Plantation

Kiplin Hall

Kiplin

Hodber Hill Plantation

122

River Swale

Rushwood Farm

Laylands Farm

121

Ellerton Hill

Manor House

Castle Hills

N

Bolton Beck

The Grange

Ellerton

airfield

0 ————— 1 Mile

0 ————— 1 Km

Scorton Beck

Bolton-on-Swale

B6271

85

A1(T)

- Bear right up across a field to a gateway and turn left beside a busy road. Cross it and the bridge over the River Swale. Brompton-on-Swale is straight ahead. Then turn right and down, immediately before road junction signs.

- The path takes you beside the River Swale, past a large pond on the left, and across a field. Go through a gate and up slightly, to a minor road; bear right. Next, turn left into Flat Lane, as signposted.

- At the B6271 turn right briefly, then left up a road which leads to St Mary's Church, Bolton-on-Swale: see panel.

- Follow the road for about 150 m, and bear right, then left beside Bolton Beck.

- Be sure to veer right to a stile. Then follow two field edge paths separated by another stile. About 200 m along the second, bear left across a tiny stone bridge to a further stile, and turn right.

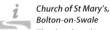

Church of St Mary's, Bolton-on-Swale

The churchyard is probably better known than the church as the location of a memorial to one Henry Jenkins. He died in 1670, reputedly at the age of 160 years. This claim was later widely discredited.

St Mary the Virgin's church was built by the abbots of St Mary of York, probably during the first half of the 14th century on the site of earlier places of worship. Fragments of a Saxon structure have survived; parts of a south door date from the 14th century and the tower was erected about a century later. The church was enlarged and restored in 1859. It is open during daylight hours and well worth a visit.

St Mary's Church, Bolton-on-Swale

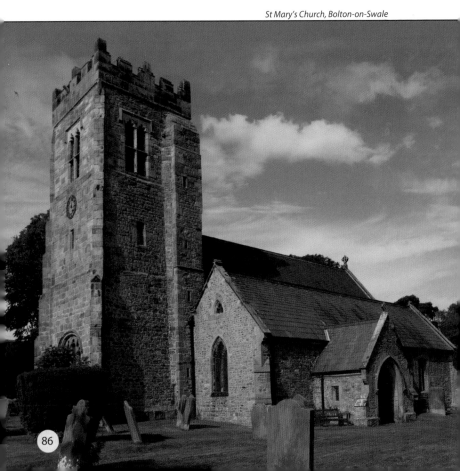

- Follow the field edge, then cross the field to a gate. Cross the minor road and go through the gate opposite.

- Continue beside Bolton Beck to a stile. Cross the road and turn left. Take the first turn right, a signposted bridleway. This minor road passes houses to reach a stile and another field edge path.

- Pass through two gates, cross the B6271 road and turn left. Using the verge where possible, follow the road, past the entrance to Kiplin Hall, for over half a mile (1 km). Just after a bend, cross to a track.

- This takes you past Ladybank House to a path beside a wood where you continue along a field edge, with a hedge on the right. Beyond a gate comes another field edge path, this time with the hedge on your left.

- Pass a ruinous building, follow a path to a small stone bridge, then another hedge-lined path. At its end, turn left along a signposted track.

- Turn right along a footpath, past Moor House. Almost immediately, go left through a gate, past farm buildings, to a stile. Bear left, then right, down a field.

- Beyond two stiles and a hedge, cross the next field to another stile and another field. Bear left across a narrow footbridge, cross a stile and turn right along the field edge.

- Bend left then right to a longer field edge path, and on to a minor road where you turn right. Take the first left turn to High Brockholme Farm.

- At a bend, go straight on over a stile beside a gate to a field edge. Then it's over a stile, and along a field edge to a gate. Turn left, then right. The path leads through a band of trees, crossing a track, en route.

- Shortly after the next gate, bear right then left through a gate. Swing right and continue down to a road where you turn left toward Danby Wiske. There's a notable church on your right before the village centre: see photographs and panel on pages 88-9.

- To continue through the village, turn right at the village green T-junction shown below.

Village green with pub, Danby Wiske

11 Danby Wiske to Ingleby Cross

Distance	**8½ miles (13.7 km)**
Terrain	**minor road, field paths, main road verge; farm tracks, field paths; crossing of busy trunk road, minor road**
Food and drink	**Danby Wiske, A19 services, Ingleby Cross**
Summary	**through fields and woodlands with wide vistas, to attractive twin villages at the foot of the North York Moors escarpment**

Danby Wiske   Oaktree Farm   Sydal Lodge   Ingleby Cross

0 km   5   10

- From the T-junction, the road leads north-east out of Danby Wiske. Just after mile 128, almost opposite a track to Lazenby Hall Farm, bear left along a field edge footpath to a track.

- In front of a band of trees, take a few steps left, then go through the trees and straight on across a field.

- Pass through a gap in a hedge and left to a field edge path. This leads to a succession of features typical of this section, generally maintaining your direction of travel: track through a hedge gap, field edge path and stile. Then turn right to another stile.

- Go up past a car sales yard to the A167 road where you turn left for 500 m past Oaktree Farm to reach a signposted turn on the right. (For Lovesome Hill Farm, with accommodation and evening meals by arrangement, continue a further 500 m along the road.)

Danby Wiske church

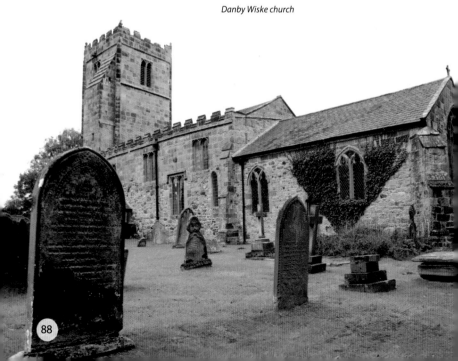

133

Hawksnest

Harsley
Grove

132

Low Moor Lane

Lingfield

Wray
House

Long Lane

131

Northfield
House
Northfield
Farm

Town
End

Deighton

Newstead
Grange

Moor
House

Deighton Lane

130

250

White House
Farm
Leascar

The
Grange

Oaktree
Hill

Lovesome
Hill

A167

Oaktree
Farm

129

A167

Crawford
Farm

Viewley
Hill Farm

London-Edinburgh

Lazenby
Grange

128

River Wiske

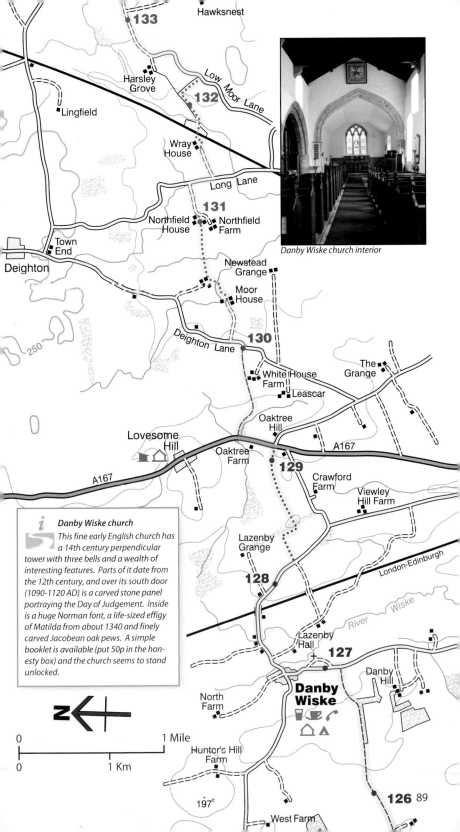

Danby Wiske church interior

i **Danby Wiske church**
*This fine early English church has
a 14th century perpendicular
tower with three bells and a wealth of
interesting features. Parts of it date from
the 12th century, and over its south door
(1090-1120 AD) is a carved stone panel
portraying the Day of Judgement. Inside
is a huge Norman font, a life-sized effigy
of Matilda from about 1340 and finely
carved Jacobean oak pews. A simple
booklet is available (put 50p in the honesty box) and the church seems to stand
unlocked.*

Lazenby
Hall

127

Danby
Hill

N

**Danby
Wiske**

0   1 Mile

0   1 Km

North
Farm

Hunter's Hill
Farm

197ft

West Farm

126 89

- Follow the track for a few hundred metres to a stile. Walk along a field edge and go over another stile to a path through trees, leading to a road.

- Bear left for a short distance to the track to Moor House. The uplands of the North York Moors now dominate the outlook ahead.

- At the farm entrance, bear left along a path to a stile and a field edge path. Go through a hedge to another such path.

- Cross a farm track and follow arrows that indicate the line to follow through another field. The next stretch is easy: across a farm track, over two stiles separated by a footbridge, and a field traverse. Beyond some more stiles you reach a farm track.

- Bear left, then right, past a house and follow a track to a minor road where you turn right. Then it's first left along a farm access track to Wray House. At the farmyard threshold, bear right over two stiles, down a field then left along its lower edge for about 100 m.

- Cross the railway with care, then follow a field path that descends to cross a stream. Field edge paths, bending right en route, bring you to Low Moor Lane.

- Turn left along the lane. Beyond Harlsley Grove, it becomes a track. Follow this to a road and turn left, then almost immediately right, along another track.

- Go straight on at Sydal Lodge over a stile to a field path. On the far side of a hedge, bear slightly right and down to a footbridge.

Water tower, Ingleby Arncliffe

- Then it's uphill to steer right and left around what's left of a brick building. Turn right along a track to the A19 services.

- Cross this very busy trunk road by its central reservation, directly to the minor road to Ingleby Arncliffe.

- The village has a splendid water tower built in 1915 by Sir Hugh Bell. At this junction, go left then right, down to Ingleby Cross.

- To reach Osmotherley, an alternative overnight stop, follow the first three bullets on page 92, but instead of turning sharp left before the gate, go straight through it and descend on the Cleveland Way southbound.

SCUGDALE

·1048"

Clain
Wood

Whorlton
Moor

Shepherd
Hill

Swainby

140

Back Lane

Scarth
Nick

Scarth
Lees

Scarth Wood
Moor

South
Wood

139

God Beck
Resevoir

Arncliffe
Wood

Beacon
Hill

Carr Beck

×mast

South
Wood

Cleveland Way
(National Trail)

Gwinestye
Hill

138

Osmotherley

Summerfield

Norwood
Farm

Arncliffe
Hall

137

Park
House

Rueberry Lane

Ingleby
Cross

Chapel Wood
Farm

Ingleby
Arncliffe

136

A172

Thorntree
Farm

Mount Grace
Priory (ruin)

Mount Lodge
Farm

250

A19

services

Grinkle
Carr

Cock Bush
Hall Farm

River Wiske

Longlands

135

Brecken
Hill (ruin)

Thornflatt

Winchatt

footbridge

Sydal
Lodge

Low
Siddle

Siddle
Grange

East
Harsley

134

Low Moor Lane

Deepdale
Farm

Thorntree

Deepdale

133

Hawksnest

Harsley Grove

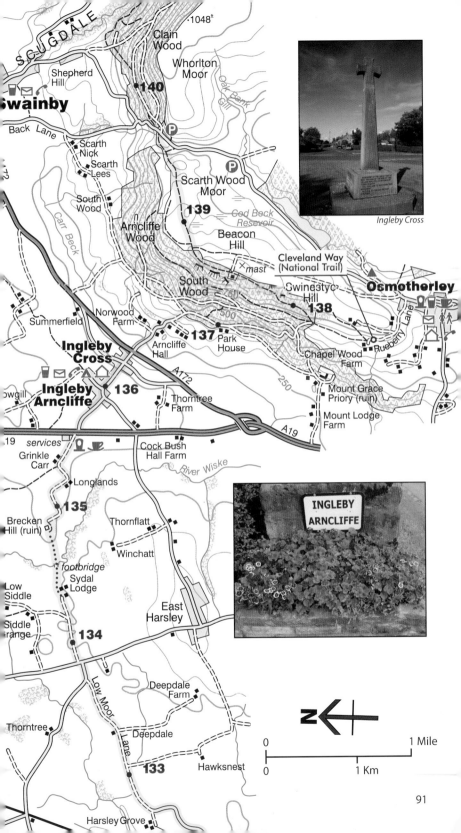

Ingleby Cross

INGLEBY
ARNCLIFFE

N

0   1 Mile

0   1 Km

91

12 Ingleby Cross to Clay Bank Top

Distance	**12 miles (19.3 km)**
Terrain	**minor road, forest paths and tracks at first, then well-drained moorland paths, paved in places, over Carlton Bank, Cringle Moor and Hasty Bank**
Food and drink	**Ingleby Cross and Carlton Bank (Lord Stones) only**
Summary	**a magnificent introduction to the rolling, heathery ridges of the North York Moors, with wide views to wooded valleys and fields**

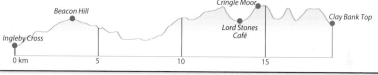

- Refer to the map on page 91: in Ingleby Cross, walk through the village, past the Cross and Blue Bell inn, and straight on along a minor road. This takes you past handsome Arncliffe Hall and up to the entrance to Cleveland Forest.

- Turn right along a forest road, gaining height steadily, to a T-junction where you turn right, soon passing Park House B&B. To visit Mount Grace Priory, turn right past Park House and walk over half a mile (1 km) south-west: see map page 91, also page 27.

- The route continues to climb and within 400 m, just short of a gate, you meet the Cleveland Way, rising from Osmotherley, 2 miles (3 km) to the south.

- Turn sharp left uphill to join the Cleveland Way northbound into the forest. In fact, you will stay with it all the way to Clay Bank Top and on to Bloworth Crossing (13 miles/21 km to the east).

North-east from the Wain Stones

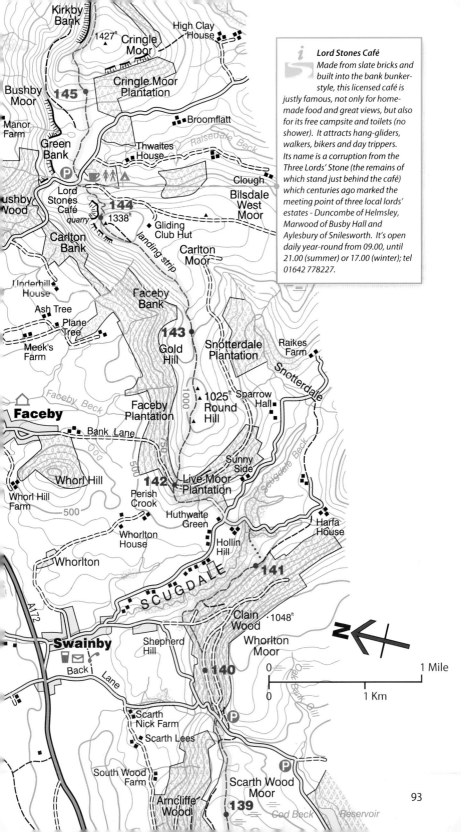

Kirkby Bank

1427ʰ Cringle Moor

High Clay House

Bushby Moor

145

Cringle Moor Plantation

Manor Farm

Broomflatt

Green Bank

Thwaites House

Raisedale Beck

Bushby Wood

P

Lord Stones Café
quarry

144

1338ʰ

Clough

Bilsdale West Moor

Carlton Bank

Gliding Club Hut

landing strip

Carlton Moor

Underhill House

Faceby Bank

Ash Tree

Plane Tree

Meek's Farm

143

Gold Hill

Snotterdale Plantation

Raikes Farm

Snotterdale

Faceby Beck

Faceby

Faceby Plantation

1025ʰ Round Hill

Sparrow Hall

1000

Bank Lane

Scugdale Beck

Whorl Hill

Whorl Hill Farm

142

Perish Crook

500

Live Moor Plantation

Sunny Side

Whorlton House

Huthwaite Green

Harfa House

Whorlton

Hollin Hill

141

S C U G D A L E

A172

Swainby

Back Lane

Shepherd Hill

Clain Wood

1048ʰ

Whorlton Moor

N

140

0 ——— 1 Mile

0 ——— 1 Km

Scarth Nick Farm

Scarth Lees

P

South Wood Farm

Scarth Wood Moor

P

Arncliffe Wood

139

Cod Beck Reservoir

i **Lord Stones Café**
Made from slate bricks and built into the bank bunker-style, this licensed café is justly famous, not only for home-made food and great views, but also for its free campsite and toilets (no shower). It attracts hang-gliders, walkers, bikers and day trippers.
Its name is a corruption from the Three Lords' Stone (the remains of which stand just behind the café) which centuries ago marked the meeting point of three local lords' estates - Duncombe of Helmsley, Marwood of Busby Hall and Aylesbury of Snilesworth. It's open daily year-round from 09.00, until 21.00 (summer) or 17.00 (winter); tel 01642 778227.

- Continue up through the forest first on a track, then on a path with Scots pines. Above the plantation, you walk through pleasant woodland dominated by birch. Pass a microwave radio station and a mast on Beacon Hill, soon descending through two gates to Scarth Wood Moor, introduced by an information panel.

- The well-made path, stone-paved in places, leads along the northern fall of the ridge to a junction. Follow the sign down to the left. A stone surfaced path, with stone wall on its left, descends to a minor road.

- Turn left for a few metres, then right along a path which soon joins a track. Next, swing left and then descend steeply to a track. Go diagonally left to a path and turn right.

- This pleasant woodland path affords good views of Scugdale. Descend left, go through a gate and across a field to another gate. Go down through more woodland to cross a stream. Turn left at a road, crossing Scugdale Beck and on to Huthwaite Green.

- Cross the road to continue along a path, climbing steeply through woodland, then more gently across moorland and up to a large cairn on Round Hill (312m/1025ft).

- Next, it's down, along and then steadily up to Carlton Moor, soon passing Carlton Moor Gliding Club with its rough landing strip and large shed. (Its splendid notice pointing out that rights of access don't extend to an aerodrome is shown on page 15.)

- There are fine views from Carlton Bank, all the way up to the trig pillar with marker stone (408m/1338ft). Inevitably it's downhill from here, steeply at first, to a road.

- Cross the road, go over a stile and follow a grassy track. The famous Lord Stones Café is nearby to the right: see panel on page 93.

- Continue past a camping ground, and a field on the right, along a wide grassy track. It leads steadily up to the summit of Cringle Moor (435m/1427ft), with its welcome stone seat and helpful view indicator: see photograph opposite. A distinctive feature in the panorama is Roseberry Topping, with its mini-Matterhorn profile, northward across the patchwork of fields and woods.

- The ensuing ascent is steep and on a mostly good path. The path crosses a gap where you ignore a possible left turn, go through a gate and bear left around the end of a stone wall and uphill.

- Beyond a gate, climb steeply to a lesser summit (402m/1317ft) then down on a steep stepped path to Garfit Gap. Gather strength for the last sharp climb of the day, up to the Wain Stones, an outcrop of large angular boulders.

- Follow the route directly through them, resisting the temptation to bypass to the left, and continue along the ridge of Hasty Bank.

- Drop downhill and turn right at a track junction, soon reaching the road at Clay Bank Top.

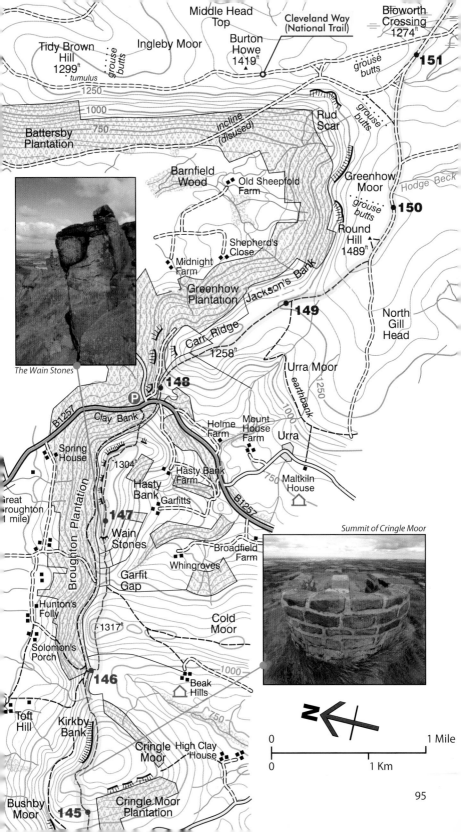

Middle Head Top

Ingleby Moor

Burton Howe 1419ft

Cleveland Way (National Trail)

Bloworth Crossing 1274ft

Tidy Brown Hill 1299ft

grouse butts

tumulus

151

grouse butts

1250

1000

Battersby Plantation

750

incline (disused)

Rud Scar

grouse butts

Hodge Beck

Barnfield Wood

Old Sheepfold Farm

Greenhow Moor

grouse butts

150

Shepherd's Close

Round Hill 1489ft

Midnight Farm

Greenhow Plantation

Jackson's Bank

North Gill Head

Carr Ridge 1258ft

149

Urra Moor

earthbank

1250

148

1000

P

Clay Bank

B1257

Spring House

1304ft

Holme Farm

Mount House Farm

Urra

750

Hasty Bank Farm

Maltkiln House

Great Broughton (1 mile)

Hasty Bank

Garfitts

B1257

147

Wain Stones

Broadfield Farm

Whingroves

Broughton Plantation

Garfit Gap

Cold Moor

Hunton's Folly

1317ft

Solomon's Porch

146

1000

Beak Hills

Toft Hill

Kirkby Bank

750

Summit of Cringle Moor

Cringle Moor

High Clay House

0 _____ 1 Mile

N

Bushby Moor

145

Cringle Moor Plantation

0 _____ 1 Km

The Wain Stones

95

13 Clay Bank Top to Blakey Ridge

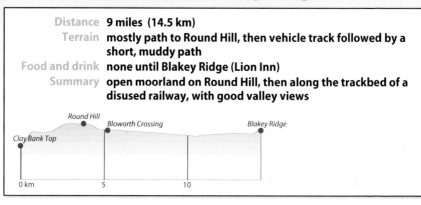

Distance	**9 miles (14.5 km)**
Terrain	**mostly path to Round Hill, then vehicle track followed by a short, muddy path**
Food and drink	**none until Blakey Ridge (Lion Inn)**
Summary	**open moorland on Round Hill, then along the trackbed of a disused railway, with good valley views**

- Refer to the map on page 95: from the road at Clay Bank Top, set out along the path to the east, and go through a gate. Climb steeply to another gate after which the path levels out, more or less. A little more ascent takes you to a large, sprawling cairn on the upper slopes of a higher Round Hill than the last.

- Continue uphill. A vehicle track soon joins from the right. About 600 m further on, you reach the flat summit of Round Hill (454m/1489ft). Opposite the trig pillar is the Hand Stone, an old waymarker on which the letters are now almost illegible. About 200 m further on stands the metre-high Face Stone, bearing a rather grim carved face.

- At a junction on the left, go straight on along a path to a track where you turn right. Pass two barriers to reach Bloworth Crossing, on the trackbed of the Rosedale ironstone railway: see panel.

Bloworth Crossing in winter

> *i* **Rosedale ironstone railway**
> The rich veins of ironstone in Rosedale had been exploited since the Iron age by the time of the 19th century industrial revolution. Large-scale mining began in 1856 and Rosedale flourished. Initially transport of the valuable, high-grade ore involved a difficult journey by road and track. Extensions of the main railway line made the construction of a more direct route to Rosedale possible and a standard gauge railway 32 km (20 miles) in length was built in 1861. Amazingly, despite winter snowstorms and blizzards, more than 10 million tons of ore were transported along the line before it was closed in 1929. It now gives Coast to Coasters 8 km (5 mi) of superbly graded, easy walking from Bloworth Crossing to near the Lion Inn.

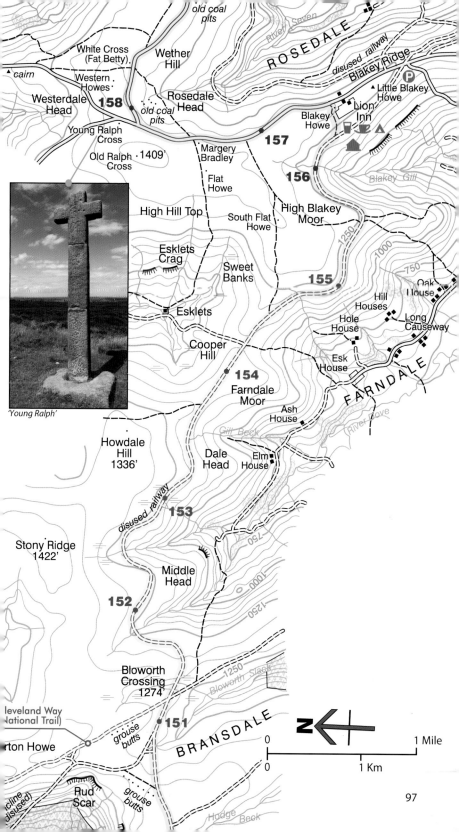

old coal pits

White Cross (Fat Betty)

Wether Hill

▲ cairn

Western Howes

Westerdale Head

158

old coal pits

Young Ralph Cross

Old Ralph Cross ·1409'

ROSEDALE

River Seven

disused railway

Blakey Ridge

▲ Little Blakey Howe

P

Blakey Howe

Lion Inn

157

Rosedale Head

Margery Bradley

Flat Howe

High Hill Top

South Flat Howe

High Blakey Moor

156

Blakey Gill

1250

1000

750

Esklets Crag

Sweet Banks

155

Oak House

Hill Houses

Hole House

Long Causeway

Esklets

Cooper Hill

Esk House

FARNDALE

154

Farndale Moor

Ash House

River Dove

'Young Ralph'

Howdale Hill 1336'

Gill Beck

Dale Head

Elm House

disused railway

153

750

Stony Ridge 1422'

Middle Head

1000

1250

152

Bloworth Crossing 1274'

1250

Bloworth Slack

leveland Way National Trail)

151

BRANSDALE

N

0 _____ 1 Mile

0 _____ 1 Km

...rton Howe

grouse butts

Rud Scar

grouse butts

...cline disused)

Hodge Beck

- The next five miles is comparatively easy walking along this disused railway. It will, with luck, be enhanced by fine views southwards across the graceful folds of partly wooded dales, Farndale and Rosedale.

- Turn left at an LWW sign on a small boulder, to follow a peaty path. LWW stands for the Lyke Wake Walk: see panel on page 99.

- Go past a stone building on the right, up and over to the road at Blakey Ridge. To continue the C2C, turn left. To visit the Lion Inn, turn right for 200 m: see panel below.

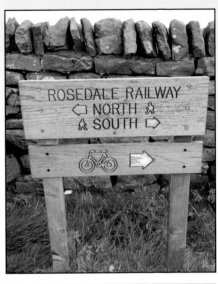

The Lion Inn, Blakey Ridge: general view (below) and wishing well (above)

i The Lion Inn

The Lion Inn, high on Blakey Moor (at 404 m/1325 ft), is a real walker's haven, whether for refreshments en route or as shelter from the rain- and windswept moors. Neolithic and Bronze Age burials show that the area has been occupied since prehistoric times. A simple inn may have existed there during the 14th century, though The Lion is traditionally dated from the 1550s. By the mid 18th century a corn market had been set up there by local farmers. The inn was extended during the 19th century but its fortunes declined when the nearby Rosedale railway closed in 1929. Widespread car ownership stimulated a revival and today the inn is seldom quiet. It's open daily from 12 noon and has 10-12 rooms for B&B. Visit www.lionblakey.co.uk, or tel 01751 417320.

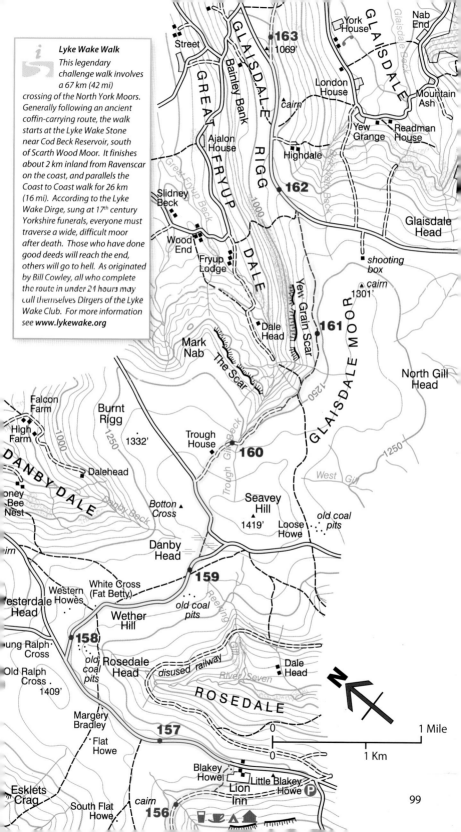

Lyke Wake Walk

This legendary challenge walk involves a 67 km (42 mi) crossing of the North York Moors. Generally following an ancient coffin-carrying route, the walk starts at the Lyke Wake Stone near Cod Beck Reservoir, south of Scarth Wood Moor. It finishes about 2 km inland from Ravenscar on the coast, and parallels the Coast to Coast walk for 26 km (16 mi). According to the Lyke Wake Dirge, sung at 17th century Yorkshire funerals, everyone must traverse a wide, difficult moor after death. Those who have done good deeds will reach the end, others will go to hell. As originated by Bill Cowley, all who complete the route in under 24 hours may call themselves Dirgers of the Lyke Wake Club. For more information see www.lykewake.org

14 Blakey Ridge to Grosmont

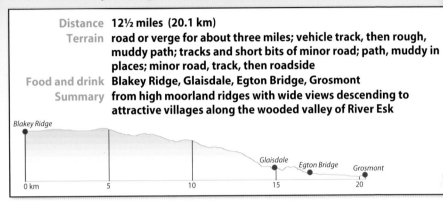

Distance	**12½ miles (20.1 km)**
Terrain	**road or verge for about three miles; vehicle track, then rough, muddy path; tracks and short bits of minor road; path, muddy in places; minor road, track, then roadside**
Food and drink	**Blakey Ridge, Glaisdale, Egton Bridge, Grosmont**
Summary	**from high moorland ridges with wide views descending to attractive villages along the wooded valley of River Esk**

- Refer to the map on page 99: follow the Blakey Ridge roads north, then east, for nearly 3 miles (5 km). Turn right at the first junction, signed for Rosedale Abbey.

- About 600 m along, you'll see Fat Betty on the left, a squat stone topped by a wheel cross, one of the figures in a colourful local folk tale: see panel opposite.

Fat Betty

- Less than a mile (1.5 km) further on, above Danby Moor, a signpost indicates a short cut by boggy path. If you stick to the road, turn left shortly, at the T-junction.

- From the path, turn left on rejoining the road, until you reach the signposted route to Glaisdale. This track passes Trough House, and soon narrows to a path, rough and muddy in places.

- Traversing the northern edge of Glaisdale Moor, you may enjoy fine views of Great Fryup Dale below. Turn left at a road beside an information panel about Danby Moors Estate, and follow it for about 600 m to a track signed to Glaisdale.

- Here and elsewhere, from early July heather carpets the moors with delicate purple. The track descends steadily towards Glaisdale. Go through a gate and continue down to a minor road into the village.

- Turn right at the next junction. Beyond a right bend, go left at a staggered junction down a narrow road marked Local Traffic Only. Descend steeply between fields and woodland, and go on up to a junction.

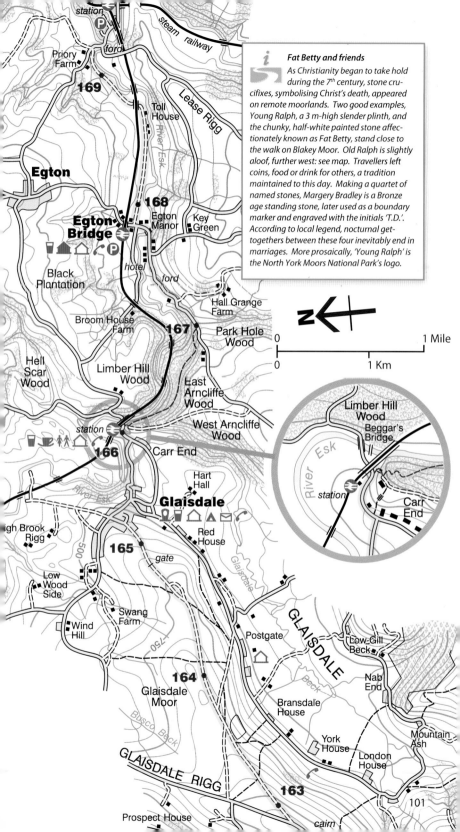

station

P

ford

steam railway

Priory
Farm

169

Lease Rigg

River Esk

Toll
House

Egton

168

Egton Manor

Key
Green

**Egton
Bridge**

hotel

ford

Black
Plantation

Hall Grange
Farm

Broom House
Farm

167

Park Hole
Wood

Hell
Scar
Wood

Limber Hill
Wood

East
Arncliffe
Wood

West Arncliffe
Wood

station

166

Carr End

Hart
Hall

Glaisdale

River Esk

gh Brook
Rigg

Red
House

165

gate

Low
Wood
Side

500

Glaisdale

Swang
Farm

Wind
Hill

Postgate

750

164

Glaisdale
Moor

Bosco Beck

Bransdale
House

GLAISDALE

Low-Gill
Beck

Nab
End

Beck

York
House

London
House

Mountain
Ash

GLAISDALE RIGG

163

Prospect House

cairn

101

i Fat Betty and friends

As Christianity began to take hold during the 7th century, stone crucifixes, symbolising Christ's death, appeared on remote moorlands. Two good examples, Young Ralph, a 3 m-high slender plinth, and the chunky, half-white painted stone affectionately known as Fat Betty, stand close to the walk on Blakey Moor. Old Ralph is slightly aloof, further west: see map. Travellers left coins, food or drink for others, a tradition maintained to this day. Making a quartet of named stones, Margery Bradley is a Bronze age standing stone, later used as a boundary marker and engraved with the initials 'T.D.'. According to local legend, nocturnal get-togethers between these four inevitably end in marriages. More prosaically, 'Young Ralph' is the North York Moors National Park's logo.

N

0   1 Mile

0   1 Km

Limber Hill
Wood

Beggar's
Bridge

River Esk

station

Carr
End

- Bear left, down to the railway station. Turn off along a path to Egton Bridge. For a good view of Beggar's Bridge nearby, go under the railway. It was reputedly built in 1619 by local lad Tom Ferris (who made a fortune at sea) to provide a safe river crossing for courting couples.

- Cross a footbridge then climb steps to a path through East Arncliffe Wood, a cool, magical place with mature trees. Muddy in places between firm stretches, the path eventually leads up to a minor road where you turn left.

- Along the road, a small footbridge bypasses a ford if need be. Cross the River Esk at the edge of the village of Egton Bridge.

- A little further on, turn off along a track to Grosmont, through the grounds of Egton Estate. The handsome manor house is partly hidden by trees on the right. Pass a toll house, with the fares charged in 1949 posted on the facing wall.

> ### North York Moors railway
> *The sound of a steam train's whistle can provide an encouraging signal that you're not far from Grosmont. The railway's history goes back to its opening in 1836 as a horse-drawn tramway between Whitby and Pickering, along a route designed by rail pioneer George Stephenson. Locomotives took over a decade later. Grosmont stands at the junction between the branch line from Pickering and that through the Esk valley between Whitby and Teeside. Declining revenues prompted closure of the Grosmont-Pickering line in 1965, but after much hard work, dedicated enthusiasts reopened the line between Pickering and Goathland in 1973 and Grosmont in 1975. Trains, most steam-hauled, operate daily between April and October; 300 volunteers keep the very successful enterprise running smoothly. For more information, visit* ***www.nymr.co.uk***.

- Go under the railway and continue down the wide, wooded Esk valley. At a road junction, cross and turn right. Go over a bridge, across the railway and on into Grosmont.

Beggar's Bridge, near Glaisdale

102

Raikes Lane

Shooting House Rigg

Newton House Plantation

Haxby Plantation

Soulsgrave Farm

Sneaton Low Moor

176

New May Beck

Belt Plantation

P

Mally Wood

Doves Nest Farm

175

Old May Beck

B1416

Thorn Hill

Falling Foss

ford

Moor House Farm

Consitt Field Plantation

Newton House

174

Falling Foss

The Hermitage

Foss Farm

Great Wood

Leas Head Farm

Littlebeck

Intake Farm

Little Beck

Hilltop Farm

173

500

Wash Beck

Low Quebec Farm

Parsley Beck Rigg

Parsley Beck

gate

750

A169

High Quebec Farm

Blue Bank

172

A169

Pen Howe Slack

Flat Howe

P

Pen Howe

Breckon Howe

Black Brow

old quarries

171

High Bride Stones

Tank engine near Grosmont

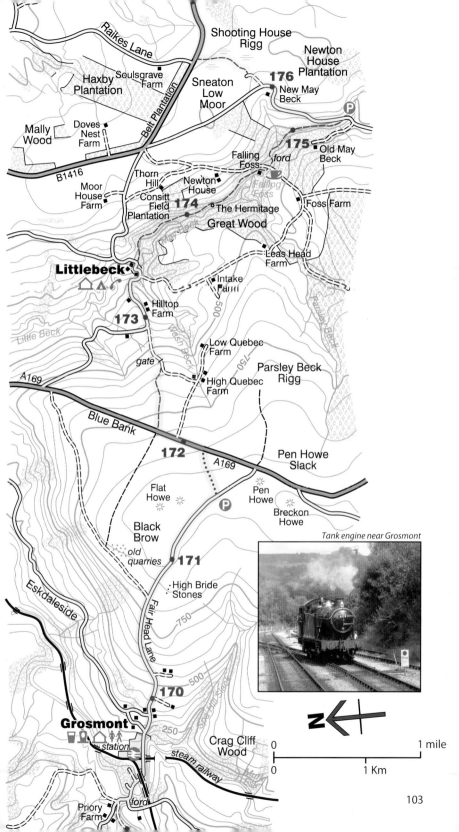

Eskdaleside

Fair Head Lane

750

Steam Hill Slack

500

170

N

Grosmont

station

Crag Cliff Wood

250

0   1 mile

0   1 Km

steam railway

Priory Farm

ford

103

15 Grosmont to Robin Hood's Bay

Distance	**14½ miles (23.3 km)**
Terrain	**minor roads, roadside verge and track; rough woodland paths, muddy in places; moorland tracks and paths; more minor road with a final 3 miles of clifftop path**
Food and drink	**Grosmont, Falling Foss, High Hawsker, Robin Hood's Bay**
Summary	**a splendidly varied day of moors, woods and scenic coastal cliffs, with the picturesque village of Robin Hood's Bay as fitting finale**

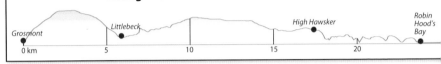

- Refer to the map on page 103: from Grosmont, head east up the main road. Its gradient is extreme, as steep as 1:3 in places. Bear right at two junctions, up toward and across the wide open moorland.

- After about 2 miles (3 km), turn left along a path to Littlebeck, boggy in places, through heather moorland.

Falling Foss

- The path descends slightly to the A169. Cross the road and turn left to walk along the verge.

- A few steps past a farm access track, turn right along a path to Littlebeck. Descend steadily to join a track from the right.

- Cross a stile to a road and go down it steeply into the tranquil hamlet of Littlebeck. Just beyond a ford is an information board about the area.

- Go steeply up, around a bend and bear right to a path through Little Beck Nature Reserve toward Falling Foss waterfall.

- The path follows a sinuous, undulating route through beautiful woodland, muddy in places with some sections relieved by duckboards.

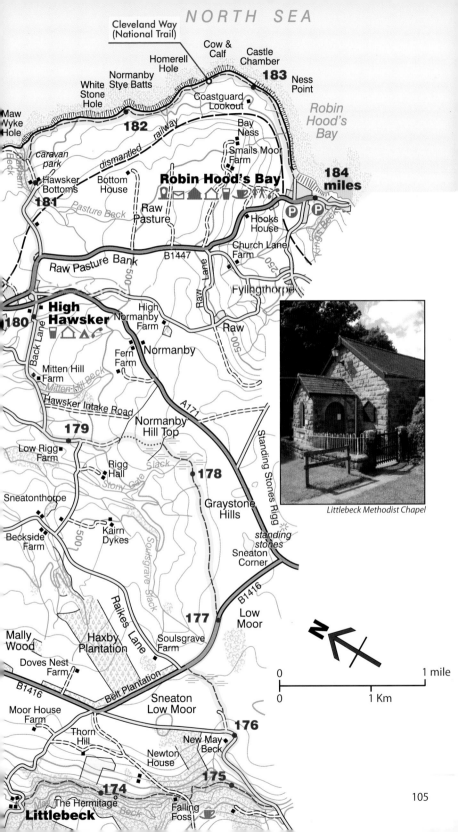

Littlebeck Methodist Chapel

- After over half a mile (1 km), you climb a long flight of steps to reach the Hermitage, a huge, hollowed out boulder with seats inside, carved for local schoolmaster George Chubb in 1754. His initials are above the entrance. Bear left and up, then right.

- At the next junction, swing right towards the waterfall, soon reaching a viewpoint. Pass or visit the splendid Falling Foss Tea Garden (normally open daily from 10.30, depending on demand). Afterwards, cross a bridge to a parking area, and walk up the access track.

- Cross a minor road to a signposted path. Follow it up and over, ford May Beck and join a wide path. Along the way, cross a footbridge and bear left at a minor junction, soon beside the stream.

- Continue up, pass through a gate and drop down, eventually to emerge into the open beside the stream. Cross to a minor road and turn left uphill.

- Shortly beyond a sharp left bend, turn right along a path to Hawsker. It's dry at first, but soon becomes boggy then wet, with decrepit duckboards providing some respite.

- Cross a stile to the B1416 road and turn right for about 800 m. At long last, the North Sea may be visible from about here. Climb over a stile, taking the path towards Hawsker.

- All too soon, the path deteriorates, though there's a stretch of duckboard. A few marker posts guide the way to a stile.

- Bear right briefly along a path, faint at best, towards a gate ahead, then veer left along a faint spur to pick up a track leading to a gate. Next, a hedge-lined, rough and muddy path leads to a minor road where you turn right.

- At the next junction (where the road is signposted to Robin Hood's Bay) bear right, then go straight ahead into the village of High Hawsker. Almost immediately, turn left then right, guided by road signs.

Towards North Cheek, with South Cheek distant at right

- Follow the roadside path. About 60 m short of a right bend ahead, cross to a signposted path between stone pillars. It bypasses the road junction and emerges on the road to two holiday parks.

- At the entrance to Northcliffe Park, turn right and follow the minor road for about 50 m, then turn left as indicated. Walk down the road between the caravans, slightly to the right.

- Just past the last caravan, cross a grassed area to a gap in the hedge and a waymarker. Follow the path down, then bear right along the cliffs.

- The undulating path provides excellent walking, mostly on a firm surface and along the cliff tops. In good visibility, pause to view the fossil-rich cliffs and at low tide, the rock platforms.

- Once you spot a white lookout building (slightly inland), look for the distant headland to its right: this is the South Cheek of Robin Hood's Bay, well beyond your destination.

- About 2 miles (3 km) after the caravan park, you reach North Cheek, also known as Bay Ness, cared for by the National Trust. After rounding the headland, you gain your first, keenly-anticipated view of Robin Hood's Bay village. (For the best view, step off the path a few metres seaward, to a small gap.)

i **Rocket posts**

This post is a replica of one used here from 1923 to 1980. Rocket posts were once common on this coastline, used as target practice by the coastguard, aiming at the post instead of a ship's mast. The rocket, attached to a light rope, was fired at the mast of a boat in distress. The rope was used to haul across a hawser (heavy rope), which carried a 'breeches buoy' – a lifebuoy with canvas shorts attached. Crew members stepped into the shorts to be winched, one by one, direct from the boat to safety. Rescue by rocket continued until it was superseded by the Sea King helicopter.

- Cross Rocket Post Field, its name celebrating the replica rocket post to your right. There's an information board after you exit the gate, on the left: see panel above.

- Continue straight along the path which narrows and passes houses, emerging through a final gate along Mount Pleasant North to reach Station Road. Turn left here and at the large car park, with Victoria Hotel on your left, bear right to follow the road down to the 'Old Village & Beach'.

- The road drops very steeply to the seafront, where you'll find the official end of the walk marked by a plaque on the Bay Hotel's Wainwright Bar on the left. Congratulations on completing a wonderful and challenging journey!

Robin Hood's Bay

THE END

COAST TO COAST WALK

ALTITUDES
(Vertical Scale Greatly Exaggerated)
The Highest point reached is Kidsty Pike, 2560' (between Patterdale and Shap)

ST BEES TO ROBIN HOODS BAY

HAND CRAFTED PLAQUES
01947 880496

The Robin Hood's Bay area has a long history, stretching back to the Bronze Age, with evidence of burials nearby. Later, Roman, then Saxon and Norse settlements came and went. Definite records date from the 16th century, when there were about 50 shore-side cottages. The origin of the name is unknown, but there is no evidence for an association with the legendary folk hero. The village is known locally simply as 'Bay'.

There's no doubt about its status as a smugglers' haven, and by the 18th century its secluded location had made it Yorkshire's busiest smuggling port. To evade the excise collectors, local people built a maze of underground hiding places with passages linking the houses.

Fishing became the mainstay of the village, with its heyday in the mid 19th century when about 170 ships were based there. A coastguard station was opened in 1822, and the first lifeboat launched in 1830. Among many heroic rescues of foundering vessels, that of 'The Visitor' in 1881 is the most celebrated. In appalling weather, teams of horses dragged a lifeboat from Whitby, a hilly 8 miles (13 km) to the north, and launched it just in time to rescue the ship's crew.

Violent storms have lashed the coast, and in 1836 the Bay Hotel was washed away, but rebuilt soon afterwards. It wasn't until the early 1950s that the present 12m-high sea wall was built.

Bay's growing popularity with visitors was boosted by the opening of the Whitby to Scarborough railway in 1885, but it was a casualty of the Beeching closures in 1965.

Robin Hood's Bay has undoubtedly benefited greatly from the popularity of the C2C walk, and continues to draw visitors attracted to its largely unspoiled old village. Its prosperity has also been helped by the development of crab grounds, their produce being regarded as the finest in the north – ideal for a celebratory feast!

Old Coastguard Station visitor centre

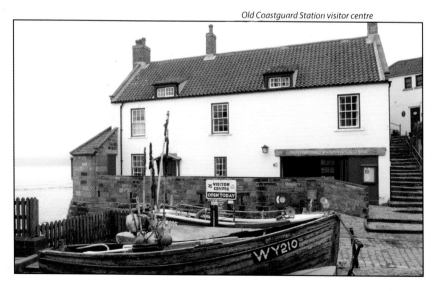

4 Reference

Further reading

Brabbs, Derry *Coast to Coast with Wainwright* Frances Lincoln, 272pp, 2009, 978-0-7112-2934-1
The ideal souvenir, by Wainwright's original collaborator

Mitchell, W R *Wainwright: his life from Milltown to Mountain* Great Northern Books, 160pp, 2009, 978-1905080663
Written by one of AW's personal friends, this has fresh insights and a wealth of anecdotes

Wainwright, Alfred *A Coast to Coast Walk: A Pictorial Guide* Revised edition, Frances Lincoln, 195pp, 2004, 0-711222-36-3
The original guidebook, with original illustrations and more recent route updates

Wainwright, Martin *The Man who Loved the Lakes* BBC Books, 192pp, 2007, 978-184-607-2947
A fine biography, coupled with some of Wainwright's favourite walks, generously illustrated

Walters, Martin *Wild Flowers* Collins Gem, 240pp, 2004, 978-00717-8544
Handy pocket size guide, excellent for identification in the field

On the three national parks

Berry, Oliver *The Lake District Travel Guide* Lonely Planet, 252pp, 2009, 978-1-7417-90917
An excellent, all-embracing introduction

Osborne, Roger and Marshall, Alan *Discover the North York Moors* North York Moors National Park Authority, 63pp, 2007, 978-1-04622-12-0
The official guide – comprehensive and abundantly illustrated

Smith, Roly and Kipling, Mike *Swaledale* Frances Lincoln, 128pp, 2008, 978-0-7112-2636-4
Well written, superbly photographed and extremely informative

Weather

www.metoffice.co.uk
Visit this website's Northwest England for Lake District National Park and specialised mountain forecast, and Yorkshire & Humber for Yorkshire Dales & North York Moors National Parks

Weathercall: Lake District & Cumbria
(*Lake District, Cumbria*) 09014 722 069, code 1903
(*Yorkshire*) 09015 722 067, code 1708

Transport information

Booking services:

www.nationalrail.co.uk	tel 08457 484 950
www.thetrainline.com	tel 0870 010 1296
www.qjump.co.uk	
www.traveline.co.uk	tel 0871 200 2233
Manchester airport	tel 08712 710 711
www.manchesterairport.co.uk	
Trans Pennine Express	tel 0845 600 1671
www.tpexpress.co.uk	
Virgin trains	tel 08457 222 333
www.virgintrains.co.uk	
Northern Rail	tel 0845 000 0125
www.northernrail.org	
National Express Coaches	tel 08717 818 181
www.nationalexpress.com	
Stagecoach Northwest Buses	tel 0871 200 2233
www.stagecoachbus.com/northwest	
Arriva Buses Northeast	tel 0870 102 1088
www.arrivabus.co.uk/northeast	
National Express East Coast	tel 08457 225 333
www.nationalexpresseastcoast.com	
Little Red Bus (Yorkshire Dales)	
www.littleredbus.co.uk	tel 01423 526 655

C2C packages and resources for independent walkers

Coast to Coast Packhorse offers car parking in Kirkby Stephen with minibus transfers to both ends of the walk, also baggage transfer (£88 for 16-day walk in 2009) and passenger service:
www.cumbria.com/packhorse tel 01768 371 777

Sherpa Van offers baggage transfer (cost £7 per day in 2009), minibus transfers (connecting both ends of walk with Darlington station, also Kirkby Stephen and Richmond) and an easy online itinerary-building service:

www.sherpavan.com

(baggage)	0871 520 0124
(accommodation)	01609 883 731

Packages with baggage transfer and accommodation booking are available from several other operators including:

Contours Walking Holidays
www.contours.co.uk tel 017684 80451
Holiday Fellowship
www.hfholidays.co.uk tel 0845 470 7558
Macs Adventure
www.macsadventure.com tel 0141 530 8886
Northwest Walks
www.northwestwalks.co.uk tel 01257 424 889
Coast to Coast Guides tel 01748 824 243
www.coasttocoastguides.co.uk
Website run by Philip Wicks of Castle Hill book shop, Richmond; it offers advice and publications, and gives online access to Doreen Whitehead's famous accommodation list.

Tourist Boards, Tourist Information Centres and National Parks

Cumbria Tourist Board   tel 01539 82 2222
www.golakes.co.uk

Yorkshire Tourist Board
www.yorkshire.com

Grasmere TIC, Redbank Road,
Grasmere, LA22 9SW;   tel 01539 435245

Kirkby Stephen TIC, Market Square,
Kirkby Stephen, CA17 4QN;   tel 01768 371199

Reeth TIC, The Library Institute, The Green,
Reeth, DL11 6TE;   tel 01748 884059

Richmond TIC, Friary Gardens, Victoria Road,
Richmond, DL10 4AJ;   tel 01748 825994

Lake District National Park Authority
www.lakedistrict.gov.uk   tel 01539 724 555

Yorkshire Dales National Park
www.yorkshiredales.org.uk   tel 0300 456 0030

North York Moors National Park
www.northyorkmoors.org.uk   tel 01439 770 657

Other useful websites

www.wainwright.org.uk

Website of the Wainwright Society (founded 2002) that celebrates AW's achievements, runs events (mainly in Cumbria), hosts forums and arranges discounts for member.

www.visitcumbria.com

A personal guide to Cumbria and the Lakes maintained by Julian Thurgood, and the source of our aerial photographs from Simon Ledingham.

Open Access Contact Centre   tel 0845 100 3298
www.openaccess.gov.uk and
www.countrysideaccess.gov.uk

St Bees
www.stbees.org.uk

Kirkby Stephen
www.kirkby-stephen.com

Richmond
www.richmond.org

Robin Hood's Bay
www.robin-hoods-bay.co.uk

Low-cost accommodation

YHA
www.yha.org.uk   (hostels)   tel 01629 592 600
     (barns)   tel 01539 431 117
Lakeland camping barns   tel 01946 758 198
www.lakelandcampingbarns.co.uk

Notes for novices

We offer advice on preparation and gear: follow the *Notes for novices* link from www.rucsacs.com. If you don't have web access, send a suitably stamped, addressed envelope to us at Landrick Lodge, Dunblane, FK15 0HY, UK.

Maps

The strip maps in this book are at a scale of about 1:50,000 and were created by Footprint:. They were updated thoroughly in mid-2009 and are also available separately as two folded waterproof sheets, at £4.95 each:
    www.footprintmaps.co.uk.

For larger-scale coverage, and for other walks near the route, Ordnance Survey maps are available from shops in the area, or online at
    www.ordnancesurvey.co.uk

Eight sheets in the 1:25,000 Explorer series are needed to cover the walk: in 2009 they cost £7.99 each. From west to east, sheet numbers are 303, OL4, OL5, OL19, OL30, 304, OL26, OL27.

Altitude profiles credit: Mapyx Ltd

The publisher thanks Mapyx for supplying all the altitude profiles from Quo, its award-winning free digital mapping software. Mapyx Quo can be downloaded free from **www.mapyx.com**

Author acknowledgements

Grateful thanks to Fran, Gordon, Hal and Jetta.

Photo credits

We thank all photographers warmly: after the page number, u means upper, l means lower.

Sandra Bardwell 10 (all 5), 12, 20u, 21u, 30, 33l, 38 (both), 39, 41, 51, 52, 55, 58, 62, 64, 69, 72 (both), 75l, 82, 84, 102, back cover; **John Burland** p25; **Steve Knell**/rspb-images.com 36; **Simon Ledingham**/visitcumbria.com 4-5, 28, 40, 42, 48, 50, 56, 57; **Jacquetta Megarry** front cover, 6, 8u, 13, 14, 15, 16, 20l, 21l, 22 (both), 27, 31u, 32u, 34 (both), 37u, 66, 67, 68 (both), 80 (both), 81 (both), 83, 85, 86, 88, 89, 90, 91 (both), 97, 98 (u and m), 100, 104, 105, 106, 107, 108 (inset), 109; **Sandy Morrison** 35l; **Andrew Parkinson**/rspb-images.com 31; **Chris Sharratt** 35u; **Gordon Simm** title, 8l, 9 (both), 17, 18, 26, 29 (both), 32l, 36u, 43, 44, 46, 54, 59, 60, 65, 70, 73, 74 (both), 75u, 76, 78 (both), 79, 87 (both), 92, 95 (both), 96, 98 (bottom), 103, 108 (main); **David Tipling**/rspb-images.com 37; **Michael Turner** 47; **Visitscotland** 33u; **Yorkshire Dales National Park Authority** 23.

Index